Rhodes Around Britain

Rhodes
Around Britain

Gary Rhodes

Photographs by Anthony Blake

BBC Books

To my wife Jenny
and my sons
Samuel and George

Acknowledgements

Thank you to everyone who has supported me during the writing of this book, and in particular: David Levin, my boss; Sue Fleming for all her advice; Anthony Blake and Joy Skipper for making the photography fun; Nicky Copeland for putting up with me; Clare Adkins for all her typing; and my *sous-chefs* and all the team. And finally, a very special thank you to my parents for their help and encouragement over the years.

Family and friends in the photographs: Stuart, Elinor and Louella Busby; Alan and Diane Jefford; Gary, Babette and Amy Oliver; Jenny, Samuel and George Rhodes; Christopher and Susan Rhodes; Keith Wyatt.

This book is published to accompany the
television series entitled *Rhodes Around Britain*
which was first broadcast in spring 1994

Published by BBC Books,
a division of BBC Enterprises Limited,
Woodlands, 80 Wood Lane
London W12 0TT

First published 1994
Reprinted, Hardback and Paperback, 1994

© Gary Rhodes 1994

Hardback ISBN 0 563 36440 8
Paperback ISBN 0 563 36995 7

Designed by Tim Higgins
Illustrations by Kate Simunek
Photographs © Anthony Blake
Styling by Anthony Blake and Joy Skipper
Food prepared by Gary Rhodes
Cutlery and crockery provided by Villeroy and Boch

Set in Monotype Ehrhardt and Ellington
by Selwood Systems, Midsomer Norton
Printed and bound in Great Britain by Butler & Tanner Ltd, Frome and London
Colour separation by Radstock Reproductions Ltd, Midsomer Norton
Jacket printed by Lawrence Allen Ltd, Weston-super-Mare
Cover printed by Clays Ltd, St Ives plc

Contents

Introduction

O, scent of the daubes [stews] of my childhood!

During the holidays, at Gémeaux, in the month of August, when we arrived in my grandmother's dark kitchen on Sunday after Vespers, it was lit by a ray of sunshine in which the dust and the flies were dancing, and there was a sound like a little bubbling spring. It was a daube, *which since midday had been murmuring gently on the stove, giving out sweet smells which brought tears to your eyes. Thyme, rosemary, bay leaves, spices, the wine of the marinade, and the fumet [bouquet] of the meat were becoming transformed under the magic wand which is the fire, into a delicious whole, which was served about seven o'clock in the evening, so well cooked and so tender that it was carved with a spoon.*

Don't you feel inspired by those words? You can see the bubbling pot, smell the richness of the sauce, and 'taste' the texture of it. Every time I read this I start to feel hungry and want to cook something. I think the late and great Elizabeth David must have felt the same, for she quoted it in her wonderful book, *French Provincial Cooking*. That was first published in 1960, and the book from which she took the quote – *Les Meilleures Recettes de ma Pauvre Mère*, by Pierre Huguenin – was published in 1936. Those words, written two generations before my own, characterize to me everything that cooking should be – full of honesty and simplicity, and using one of the finest, possibly *the* finest, techniques of cookery, good old-fashioned stewing. I'm sure somewhere in France today there are still *daubes* bubbling in pots until the meat is so tender it can be carved with a spoon. And that's the difference between the French and the British: the French have never forgotten their traditions.

So what happened to us? Was it that the traditions weren't strong or numerous enough? Or that we just didn't have the passion for food and cooking that we associate with the French and Italians? Probably, on reflection, a combination of all these.

OPPOSITE
*I've always enjoyed creating a stir with
my cooking.*

British cookery had always been simple – with wonderful ingredients like our own beef, which didn't need anything more fancy than just roasting. The British always wanted everything to taste of exactly what it was, so there were no rich complementary sauces, or tricksy combinations of foods. It was a question of featuring the main ingredient and achieving the very best taste with it. Perhaps when nothing much had changed for hundreds of years, the passion for the dish and for the art was lost.

Our cooking by the early to mid 1970s consisted of well-done roast beef, soggy Yorkshire puddings, mostly served with over-cooked cabbage and thick, floury gravy. It was when *nouvelle cuisine* hit these shores that I believe we finally lost the confidence in our own traditions and techniques, and dropped them in favour of the new ideas. The principles of the new cooking (the literal translation of *nouvelle cuisine*) had already existed in France for many years. The most renowned of modern French chefs, Fernand Point, had led a whole brigade of famous chefs – Paul Bocuse and Alain Chapel among them – away from the heavy and tyrannical traditions of classical French cookery as characterized by Escoffier. Point believed – as we in Britain once did – that flavour was of prime importance, that chicken should taste of chicken, and needn't be disguised.

However, we first encountered *nouvelle cuisine* in the form of *cuisine minceur*, food for slimmers and for health introduced by Michel Guérard, the three-Michelin-starred chef of Eugénie les Bains. We made a mistake yet again. Instead of embracing the true principles of the new French cooking, we thought the Guérard alternative was what it was all about – light, pretty, and not very much of it. We dropped everything that was British and combined all sorts of new flavours and ingredients to make small pictures on large plates, to make a riot of colour rather than big tastes. (The roast beef, stews and dumplings became foods to feed the staff!)

British chefs copied the Troisgros brothers' modern classics, such as duck breasts with blackcurrants. Fish would be served with two or three different sauces, and decorated with half a dozen sprigs of chervil or chives. Looking back at that *nouvelle* period, I can remember that, for most chefs, cooking consisted of pan-fried medallions of pork, veal or beef, or chicken breasts, served with kiwi fruit or raspberries.

Sadly, a lot of this still exists now, but I think we needed something new. We needed to think again about the flavours and textures of foods, and to reconsider our presentation – never one of our strong points. I certainly passed through this phase, believing I was a culinary artist, and that tiny crayfish garnishing each fish dish was the ultimate in modern cookery.

However, we'd missed the boat in more than one way. Even in the Troisgros' books and restaurant, the old dishes still existed alongside the new. They still cooked their boiled bacons and hams, and beef and lamb stews, whereas we had foolishly left all that behind. They still cherished their traditions. And it is those basic methods of classic cookery – whether French or British – that I believe are the essence of good cooking, and they are the backbone of my cooking today. Many other chefs in Britain have been re-assessing their own basic skills and their own heritage, but too many are still over-elaborating. Good food doesn't need elaboration. Good tastes simply need loving care.

Early Days

So how did I come to cooking? Well, as a young boy, I'd never thought of becoming a chef. I'd always wanted either to play for Manchester United (who doesn't?) or be a policeman. They say that most things start in the home. Well, that's exactly where it all started for me.

I must have been about fourteen or fifteen at the time. Because my mother and older brother, Christopher, were at work all day, someone had to look after my younger sister, Cheryl, during the school holidays, and it was up to me. And so the cooking started: something simple for lunch, a sandwich perhaps (I was hooked on cheese, tomato and pickle for years!), and something more filling for tea, or vice versa.

We'd always been brought up on good home cooking – home-made pies, roasts, stews and even a lovely corned beef hash. In fact, I think most people were then; there certainly wasn't the variety of ready-prepared foods we have now. My mother always insisted on fresh meat and vegetables, and her stews were the ones I remembered when reading the quote at the beginning, to be followed by her *pièce de résistance*, sherry trifle.

My cooking was a lot more basic – every now and again it would even be a tinned steak and kidney pie. My first real dish was shepherd's pie: cooked mince with carrots, onions and gravy topped with mashed potatoes – a complete meal. It became a regular favourite, with a few additions – baked beans or peas, and the potatoes topped with sliced tomatoes and glazed with grated Cheddar until golden brown. It was delicious; a very ordinary, everyday meal, but it gave me the inspiration to want to cook.

Another early passion was for my Uncle George's toasted cheese sandwiches. We've been trying for years to get the exact recipe out of him, but he's guarding the secret closely. Basically, it was grated onion and cheese, some mayonnaise to bind, with black pepper and mustard, I think, spread on toast and grilled. The taste was sensational, and very much another part of my culinary childhood. I would always try to re-create the sandwich at home; it was never quite the same, but those memories probably led me on to using a Welsh rarebit topping with smoked haddock. (I'm still very keen on toasted sandwiches as well.)

*A real bonus for
a chef: eating
and drinking with
friends.*

So the next move was to cook for the whole family, and what could have been better than the traditional Sunday lunch? Roast beef, lamb or pork with roast potatoes and fresh vegetables: this was quite a tall order – and on top of that a pudding! The first pudding I made was a steamed lemon sponge with lemon sauce. I'd taken the recipe from one of my mother's cookery books and followed it step by step: weighing everything, stirring, folding, re-stirring, tasting, checking all the time. In one of today's modern food processors it would probably be all mixed and made in two or three minutes, but I doubt I would have been so proud and happy with the result.

The pudding was a huge success: a light sponge with a sharp lemon taste, and a warm, rich sauce. When you make a dish for the first time and it works, it never seems to work or taste as well on the second, third or any other attempt. We all think that the first one is in a league of its own.

I'm sure that lemon sponge changed my mind about being a policeman and I was certainly never going to make it as a footballer! It was cooking that I wanted to do. But how was I to go about it?

The First Steps

I didn't have the remotest idea. So my mother and I investigated over a few weeks and we heard about Thanet Technical College in Broadstairs, which was about three-quarters of an hour by train from our home in Gillingham. I applied for a general catering course which would teach me about kitchens, restaurants and management, giving me a lot more choices in the industry.

I was interviewed and accepted. It was 1976, I was sixteen years old, and ready to go. The new students were easy to spot – floppy chef's hats, trousers three inches too long and aprons so crisp they could stand up on their own! It really was quite frightening; you know nobody and virtually nothing. In one of my first lessons, we were asked what a béchamel sauce was. Well, I didn't have a clue, but quite a few hands went up. One in particular belonged to Martin, who seemed to know a lot more than most of us, and he soon became the natural leader of the class.

As time went by, I realized that cooking was all I wanted to do, and as I learned more, my confidence grew. Towards the end of my first year, I wanted to lead the class and was determined to get there. Second best wasn't going to be good enough.

The style of cooking taught at Thanet was very traditional, very Escoffier, but I shall always value those three years. It was there that I learned all the basics that are so important to good, creative cooking – the stocks, sauces, the braising, pot-roasting and stewing, etc. – and I don't think I could have had a better training. It was there, too, that I learned how to make ingredients work together to create the flavours and smells that are the foundation of delicious dishes.

To boost my confidence during that first year, I took over virtually all the cooking at home, and I still remember cooking my first Christmas lunch for the family. It was all very traditional – turkey, chestnut stuffing, bread sauce, gravy and vegetables. I was a little more adventurous with some of the potatoes, mashing them and piping them into little nests filled with Provençale tomatoes. I made my own Christmas pudding as well, and it was all a huge success. I felt such a great sense of achievement.

After a couple of terms at college, the class was divided up into groups, each to have a speciality and each to have a leader (a *chef de partie* in the professional kitchen). I was put on to the sauce section, and I was the leader. There I was, full of myself, telling everyone what to do, and my course was set.

Things were looking up in other directions, too. My mother had happily re-married (I later gained another sister, Anna), and in my second year I began cooking dinner parties for them and their friends. I'd got a little more ambitious by then, and my favourite dish was pheasant *à la Souvaroff*. The bird was stuffed with pâté instead of the foie gras and truffles, then pot-roasted in brandy and Madeira in an earthenware dish sealed with a flour and water paste. When that seal was broken, the smell was immense, very rich and absolutely delicious. I would follow that with *omelette à la norvégienne* (baked Alaska) or *crêpes Suzette* – nothing simple! I liked the first especially – sponge, fruit and ice-cream topped with meringue and baked only until the meringue had become golden and set. I would put a little dish on top filled with cherries in Kirsch and flambée them. The tastes were there, and so were the flames, so it was re-christened omelette Vesuvius!

My parents' friends must have been impressed because soon I was cooking for them. I loved the pressure – the food had to be right, the timing had to be right. Best of all, I was learning and gaining confidence, achieving a sense of self-worth. This reflected in my work in college, and I started to do a lot better – so much so that at the end of my second year I was the student of the year, and one of my ambitions was already fulfilled.

My next ambition was to be selected for the third-year advanced cookery course, and I was. For the first time I used things like beef fillet and *foie gras*. I was taught how to recognize textures, tastes, seasonings and the richness of finished flavours. The tutors were really passionate about their cooking, and if you showed enthusiasm you were given all the help you needed. I learned a bit about sugar work, too, and how to bake bread, and widened my repertoire considerably. We all entered cookery competitions (a sort of culinary olympics), and did well, and we thought we were the *crème de la crème*. I was even more convinced of my starry future when I'd finished the course. Not only did I pick up the chef of the year award, but also the student of the year award. Perhaps the most important acquisition from college was my wife, Jenny. She couldn't bear me for the first couple of years, then eventually came to her senses! We've been together since 1979, but only married in 1989 – we had to be sure . . . .

To sum up, those years at Thanet gave me all the basic knowledge I needed to enable me to pursue my career successfully. It was because of those years that I'm cooking what I'm cooking today. I've since been through all the trends and fashions – been there, seen it and done it – but I've only 'come home' again, in a way.

My First Job

I left college with all those awards under my belt, feeling the world was my oyster. In my very first job, I was to discover that I had a lot more to learn!

All the lecturers had suggested we go to the Savoy, the Berkeley, Claridges and all the other top London hotels. However, I was determined to go abroad. The really famous names at the time were Bocuse, Guérard, Troisgros, Chapel etc., and the cookery world had begun to be dominated by *cuisines nouvelle*, *minceur*, *gourmande* etc., all coming from France. I wrote off to many famous chefs, hotels and restaurants throughout France, and I've still got all the 'thanks but no thanks' letters.

I decided that working for a hotel group might be one way of getting myself to foreign parts, so I wrote to many Hiltons throughout Europe. Amsterdam was the first to say yes, and although Paris and Zurich also offered me places, I'd already accepted the Dutch offer. So off I went to Amsterdam, leaving behind Jenny and my friends, and thought to myself – here I am, ready to show them all.

Working in a top-class hotel restaurant kitchen was a revelation. On my second day there, I found produce that I'd never seen or even heard of – kiwi fruit, finger bananas, yellow, black and white peppers, and all the varieties of wild mushrooms – and although I'd never seen a fresh truffle before, now they were arriving in virtual lorry-loads daily. I was learning all over again. Should I have ever *been* to college, or just started from scratch in a kitchen such as this? It's only now that I've realized that if I hadn't been to college, I would have a very limited range of skills. I would know how to grill, pan-fry, poach perhaps – all methods of the modern *nouvelle* kitchen – but I doubt I would have seen all the basics which are so important to me now.

The Amsterdam Hilton's newest *commis* (chef's assistant) really thought that he should be a *chef de partie* (he *had* been chef of the year at college, after all), but he soon realized why he wasn't. I was put in the larder, on the starter section for the first few days, and then it was on to the coffee shop. This was busy all day. On my own, I turned out mixed salads galore, *croques-monsieurs* by the dozen, untold numbers of club sandwiches as well as all the Dutch specialities – smoked eel salad, soused herrings and *uitsmijters* (buttered slices of bread topped with cheese, ham or beef, and finished with fried eggs). You are always under pressure on this section. The orders keep coming and you've got to keep running. But I would never accept any help; I had to do it on my own. A club sandwich wasn't going to beat me. However, the chef seemed happy, and so was I.

Things were going well, I was moving from section to section, and the hotel was almost Thanet College all over again. Jenny had joined me, Martin had arrived, and eventually there were five of us there.

After about a year, we had a new head chef, Graham Cadman, who was to be a great influence on me. I told him I wanted to be a *chef de partie* instead of a *commis*. He listened, but he made me work for it. I was put in charge of the sauce section, but still with the rank and pay of a *commis*, and 'tested' for three months. I got the job, and happily stayed on for another year.

Nouvelle cuisine was at its height then, and we would get quite carried away, often making dishes up as we went along. We garnished everything in sight, and painted as many pictures on plates as there were Dutch masters in the Rijksmuseum. We thought we were sensational.

After two and a half years, a move seemed in order, so both Jenny and I approached and were accepted by the new Hilton Hotel in Strasbourg. We were due to start there in March 1982, but when a friend asked me to join him at a new restaurant opening in Bournemouth, I changed my mind. All I could see was superstardom at home. (I *was* still only twenty-one or so, after all!)

Back in Britain

After a couple of months in this new restaurant, I started to wish I'd listened to Graham Cadman's warnings. Things weren't going to work, so it was time to move on again.

Where was I going to go? What was I going to do? My mother came up with a suggestion.

OVERLEAF
The working kitchen.

'The Connaught's the place to be,' she said, so I wrote to Michel Bourdin. It worked. He offered me the job as *demi-chef de partie*. I was delighted. My brother then told me of a job at the Reform Club in Pall Mall. At twenty-one, I knew I wasn't ready for a *sous-chef*'s job, but I thought I'd take a look anyway. I got it, and turned down the Connaught (silly boy). I was far too young, but I liked the challenge. Jenny started with me, and we stayed there for about a year.

For the first couple of months there was no head chef, so I was cooking squab pigeons with wild strawberries and chervil, all kinds of mousses and fruit plates. They looked lovely, but didn't really eat well at all. I constantly sought out those sweetnesses which every English chef seemed to think characterized *nouvelle*. A new head chef arrived, Mark Streeter, and he brought us back to real cooking. I was reminded of asparagus, tripe and onions, braised chump chops and all those basic skills which I'd neglected over the previous few years. Even though it might have seemed mad to have turned down the Connaught, the Reform Club got me thinking again.

My next step was brief, but had its effect. One of the vegetable suppliers at the Reform told me about a job going in a restaurant in Coptic Street called Winston's Eating House. I went there as head chef. The food was very English – steak and kidney puddings, sausages and mash etc. – but I was still playing with nouvelle salads with mangetouts and beans, or crayfish and artichokes, and other tricksy dishes. It was a mixture of many things. It was good, too, to make steak and oyster pies, summer puddings and beef stews. Jenny was with me and Martin joined us. There were five of us ultimately, with me running the show. It was all very exciting.

Another of the vegetable suppliers at Winston's told me he was coming to eat, and was bringing as his guest Brian Turner, chef at the Capital Hotel in Knightsbridge. I didn't have a clue who he was, but after a few ventures into food guides, I was on cloud nine. The Capital had a Michelin star, one of the few restaurants in Britain with that accolade, and Brian Turner became an instant hero. When he came, he obviously enjoyed his meal, but I must admit he looked a little suspicious when I appeared in earrings and Duran Duran haircut.

A few days later Brian Turner asked me to go and meet him. He said his *sous-chef* was leaving and that he would like me to think about taking the job. An answer in a couple of days would be fine. Two days later I accepted the job.

From Capital to Country

Things were really looking up, and I think it was then that everything began to change for me. It was all still full of surprises, too. The first person I met in the Capital kitchen was Mark Clayton, a *sous-chef* who had been at Thanet. I didn't know him then, but we recognized each other instantly, and have since become the closest of friends.

It was 1983, *nouvelle* was still flourishing, and here I was joining a Michelin-starred restaurant. I expected to find pretty pictures on plates, but it was good, honest French cooking – best end of lamb roasted with a herb crust, and *dauphinoise* potatoes: the lamb was cooked to perfection, with a crisp crust, and the potatoes had just the right texture. This was real cooking, and that people wanted to eat it was proved by the numbers of diners who returned again and again to enjoy the same things.

I stayed at the Capital for about eighteen months, and that, too, was an extremely valuable time. Brian Turner's cooking was probably the most reliable and real cooking around then, and he taught me that the simplest of foods and techniques can result in classy flavours. I also learned from him how to *run* a kitchen, and that it could be a happy place, not one ruled purely by temperament.

I then ventured into a new restaurant opening in Essex, and tried to bring the Capital to the country. I stayed about a year, but began to feel out of touch, so I returned to Brian. While there, I was told of a head chef's job in Taunton, at the Castle Hotel. I was put in touch with Kit Chapman and he asked me to meet him one day at the Inn on the Park in London. He owned the Castle and his head chef, Chris Oakes, was leaving. We met at three one Saturday afternoon, and were still talking enthusiastically about food and the future at seven in the evening – is this a record for an interview? The first question was the testing one: 'How would you feel, Gary, about putting Lancashire Hot-pot on the menu at the Castle?' To be honest, I was a little shocked – a hot-pot in a Michelin-starred restaurant? It didn't sound quite right, but I thought quickly, and said, 'Yes, of course, I would, it's a great classic dish.' It was the right answer, and I got the job. By the early evening, we'd virtually got the whole lunchtime and dinner menus planned.

Before starting in Taunton, Kit organized for me to work with Peter Kromberg at the Inter-Continental Hotel in London. It was only for a couple of weeks, but gave me an insight into the running of a large hotel. I'm convinced he is the master of executive chefs in hotels, the whole operation ran so smoothly.

It was June 1986 when I started. There were already a few Great British Classics on the menu, and I was there to take over and keep them going. It wasn't easy, but as time went on, I became convinced this was the direction in which to be moving. These dishes were so exciting, and for me the revival of braising, stewing and pot-roasting had truly begun.

That Michelin star was quite a responsibility. I feel you are obliged to produce what *they* want, not necessarily what you or the customer want. So we kept lobster, venison, sea bass and fillet of beef dishes on the *à la carte* dinner menus, and ventured wholeheartedly into the British dishes at lunchtimes. We had a different roast every day, and plenty of daily British specials – calves' liver and bacon, salmon fish cakes, steak and kidney pudding and, of course, bread and butter pudding.

I loved it all, and it wasn't just the dishes that changed. This was my first real head chef post, and so I was able to take a look at the very essence of all our cooking, the making of the stocks and sauces. It's something I learned then, and I now always teach it to the keen young cooks coming into my kitchen. A good stock is not made just by throwing bones and vegetables into a pan and boiling in water for a couple of hours; that will have some flavour, but will probably be cloudy and lack texture and the real depth of flavour necessary. I slow-roasted halves of unpeeled onions until their juices and sugars caramelized, and used these as the basis for the stock. The idea wasn't new, but I'd improved on the quick searing of an onion, which can lead to bitter flavours. My basic stock was born, and it soon became a three-day event, and still is.

I thought in Taunton that I had achieved everything I'd wanted. I was a Michelin-starred chef (I'd retained the star), and I had Jenny and our first son, Samuel (later to be joined by George). I'd also enjoyed the trip of a lifetime, arranged by Graham Cadman, my old chef from Amsterdam. I cooked braised oxtail and mashed potato in the searing heat of Singapore for two weeks as a promotion – and they loved it!

On my return to England, it was still the British Revival that interested me. Once again outside circumstances were to lead to my next move. The Chapman family were looking to sell the hotel, and I wasn't going to stay after they'd gone. At a function in London I met David Levin, who owned and had been my boss at the Capital. He knew about the Castle plans, and asked what I was going to do. I wasn't sure, and he replied, 'You never know, Gary, it may lead you straight back to me.' With Phillip Britten running the Capital, that left the Greenhouse restaurant in Mayfair, where Jenny had been *sous-chef* while I was at the Capital. It had been open for some fourteen or fifteen years, and was very busy, and I was offered the position of head chef. I was a little dubious at first – did I really want to come back to London? Did I want to be cooking for so many people each day? However, what really sealed the whole arrangement for me was that the boss wanted exactly what I wanted to do, to return to honest, basic food – the revival of the Great British Classics.

Back in London

With completely new kitchens and a new menu, we opened. The Great British Classics – faggots, fish cakes, boiled bacon, cod and parsley, oxtails – were back in town. We have enjoyed an amazing success. In 1991, we were voted *The Times*' Restaurant of the Year by one of my favourite food writers, Jonathan Meades. He always writes about what he finds and feels, which is exactly the way that I cook. He had already eaten my food at the Castle, and I just knew, when I saw the order in the Greenhouse kitchen for faggots as a starter, followed by braised oxtail and bread and butter pudding, that it had to be him! The fact that he was testing my faggots again confirmed to me that, once having achieved a high standard, that standard has to be maintained and developed.

And that's what I've been striving for ever since. The core of my menu will aways be the same five or so of my dishes, my signature dishes. I always want people to come back time and time again to eat those dishes because they like them, and because they are so consistent. The pressed duck at Le Tour d'Argent in Paris is probably the most famous dish in France, so why shouldn't my faggots or oxtails be the talk of London? Consistency, I truly believe, is the real key to success.

These dishes are mostly British in origin, and I'm proud of the part I've played in reviving them. There's a huge tradition out there, from north to south, and east to west, and the ingredients to match it. The dishes are honest and simple, with real and delicious flavours – much more satisfying to cook than a pan-fried chicken breast or veal medallion. They're also economical, because I believe you don't have to save or spend a fortune to eat good food. That's another one of my 'rules': along with simple dishes and honest flavours, you must offer value for money.

Neither does good eating involve constantly dreaming up new ideas. You should cook what you believe in, and what you enjoy. This will surprise a few other chefs, but I'm not afraid of putting baked beans on toast on the menu, or hamburgers and onions. They're all home-made, of course, and I believe that's what people want – something simple, something they know they like, something they know their *children* will like. I've even made the infamous knickerbocker glory, but all I've really done is arrange what

OVERLEAF
My two young chefs, Samuel, right,
and George, left.

other chefs might call *Assiette de sorbet de framboises et glace de vanille au coulis de fruits rouges* in a glass instead of like a picture on a plate. And it's much more fun to eat!

I don't just stop at British dishes. A lot of my favourite recipes are French, Italian and Eastern in origin, as most of them are just too good to ignore. There's the French *confit* of duck and *crème brûlée* (although some food historians would insist that the latter was originally Britain's 'burnt cream'), Italian *carpaccio* of beef, *risotto* and *gnocchi*, and Mediterranean cod *brandade* and *tapenade*. These, I think, are part of the same national culinary traditions as British dishes.

Cooking has been a passion for me ever since my teens, and I do believe that to do it well you have to do it from the heart. You have to look at what's available – the produce – and be inspired by it. In Britain, everybody should be so inspired, because there are so many delicious ingredients: the fish from Scotland, the puddings and sausages of the north, the cheeses and pasties from the west, the fruits of the east and the lamb of the south. I think we should revive scrumping for fruits! Well, perhaps not, but when we've bought a couple of pounds of damsons, apples or cherries, instead of eating them just as fruits, why not save some and make them into a home-made pie, and serve it with thick double cream. It's going to be a lot tastier than buying a ready-made pie – and so much cheaper as well.

Over 90 per cent of the recipes in this book are perfectly easy to prepare at home and they use ingredients which are readily available. I hope that they will help inspire you to cook, and that they will make producing delicious dishes much less hard work. I've explored many avenues during my career, but I'm now wedded to the many interesting culinary roads that are our heritage in Britain. Bread and butter pudding, for instance, has become a classic of today, but it was always made from the waste of yesterday. So remember, let's not lose what has been achieved, let's revive what has been lost.

Good luck.

GARY RHODES

Notes on the Recipes

1 Follow one set of measurements only, do not mix metric and imperial.

2 Eggs are size 2.

3 Wash fresh produce before preparation.

4 Spoon measurements are level.

5 A tablespoon is 15 ml; a teaspoon is 5 ml.

6 If you substitute dried for fresh herbs, use only half the amount specified.

7 Mixed herb tea bags are readily available and can be used as an alternative to bouquet garni.

8 Unless otherwise stated, 'season' or 'seasoning' simply means seasoning with salt and pepper.

9 For information on alternative recipes for Veal *Jus* and stocks, see page 225.

10 If shallots are not available, substitute with double the quantity of onions.

Soups, Starters and Snacks

This first chapter contains a wide variety of dishes, several of which could even be served as main courses for lunch or supper. Many of the soups, for instance, are quite filling and, eaten with some chunky bread, would make good and satisfying meals on their own.

ABOVE *The Rhodes 'Open' Club Sandwich (see p. 64).*
LEFT *Tomato Soup served with croûtons (see p. 30), Cabbage Soup with Dumplings (see p. 31), and the ingredients for Ham and Vegetable Soup (see p. 32).*

27

Perhaps the first thing you'll notice about my recipes is that the titles are very basic and simple. This continues throughout the book because far too often, I think, recipes are described as if they were a book. My Chicken Liver Parfait would probably read elsewhere as 'A mousse of light chicken livers spiked with garlic and brandy, bound with cream, on crisp bread with wilted green leaves and a compote of grapes, apples and onions.' If I read that, my imagination would probably run riot, visualising a towering dish with every item perfectly placed and looking as if a food Meccano set was used to build it! The reality might be a little disappointing.

None of the recipes are engraved in stone, and you can easily adapt them to your own taste. The Tomato Soup is simple enough already, but if you don't like bacon, then just leave it out. I like using the bacon because, when cooking it with the onion and vegetables, it gives a wonderful smoky flavour and yet another taste to the soup. The croûtons are an optional extra as well, adding a crunchy texture. The usual way of making these is to fry them in oil, but they're delicious and much healthier if you bake them with a little olive oil in a moderate oven for about ten minutes, turning every so often. They become golden all over and much crisper. For a little extra taste, roll them in grated Parmesan while still hot.

You can use ordinary tomatoes, but do try to find the plum tomatoes that are becoming more available in greengrocers and supermarkets. Most come from Italy, Spain or America, and are much better for cooking and eating. They have a lot lower water content than most tomatoes; squeeze one in your hand (make sure you've bought it first!), and you'll be left with a thick tomato pulp. If you did that to an ordinary tomato, you'd be left with virtually nothing. Plum tomatoes, when cooked, are packed with flavour, but if you can only find ordinary tomatoes, add a little tomato purée to compensate – the soup will still be good.

Tomatoes, in fact, are a bit of a passion of mine, and I use them a lot in these recipes. If they're good and tasty, they can add a wonderful Continental flavour to our own classic ingredients. For instance, I love buying our British mackerel and herring – so great to look at in fishmongers, piled high on crushed ice – and mackerel can take on some wonderful tastes with stewed tomatoes, onions and pesto. Grilled sardines on toast with tomatoes are just as good. The tomatoes just lift the dishes to new heights with new tastes.

I usually choose my starter after I've picked my main course to help balance the meal, but sometimes I don't worry at all and just eat whatever I fancy. I think you'll find quite enough to choose from here, most of which are French or Italian, certainly Mediterranean, in influence. These can balance the very British main courses, but there are, of course, a few of our own ideas as well.

After all, you can't get much more British than Cabbage Soup with Dumplings. The inspiration for this particular version was my stepfather John, who loves cooking, and influenced us quite a lot at home. Most Sundays we would have cabbage as a vegetable, simply boiled, seasoned and tossed in butter. Well, there's nothing wrong with that, but John decided it needed a boost. He first tossed some onions and bacon in butter, then added a little chicken stock and threw in the cabbage. It cooked very quickly and had so much more flavour, so I just added more stock and created a soup! The dumplings finish it all off. The dumpling recipe I've given is fairly basic, but can be given a lot more variety by adding garlic, bacon or mixed herbs.

Perhaps the most British dish here is the Great British Breakfast offered as a starter salad. Well, why not? Lots of delicious tastes together: the sautéed potatoes, black pudding, bacon and poached eggs with some fresh green leaves. Now that really is variety.

Tomato Soup

This soup stands up as both a starter or a main course (see pp. 26–7). It has a chunky texture and draws on all the flavours of the ingredients. The real beauty, of course, is how simple it is to make. I always like to serve it with bread croûtons cut from a loaf of crusty or olive bread and then fried or baked in olive oil. Also, fresh Parmesan flakes (done with a potato peeler) sprinkled over the soup are really delicious, but of course all these bextras are really up to you. This soup can make a great vegetarian dish – simply leave out the bacon and replace the chicken stock with a vegetable stock.

SERVES 6–8

3 onions, chopped
3 carrots, cut into 6 mm (¼ in) dice
3 celery sticks, cut into 6 mm (¼ in) dice
50 ml (2 fl oz) olive oil
25 g (1 oz) unsalted butter
½ bunch of fresh basil, chopped
½ bunch of fresh tarragon, chopped
1 bay leaf
1 large garlic clove, crushed

6 smoked back bacon rashers, rinded
   and chopped
900 g (2 lb) ripe tomatoes, preferably
   plum
600–900 ml (1–1½ pints) Chicken Stock
   (see p. 228)
Salt and freshly ground white pepper
Tomato purée (optional, to taste)

Sweat the chopped onions, carrots and celery in the olive oil and butter for a few minutes, then add the herbs, bay leaf and garlic and cook for a few more minutes. Add the bacon and continue to cook for about 5 minutes until the vegetables are slightly softened.

Cut the tomatoes into quarters and then cut again into eight pieces. Add them to the vegetables, cover the pan and cook gently for about 15 minutes. The cooking will create its own steam and slowly cook the tomatoes. The mixture must be stirred occasionally, which will help the tomatoes to break down and start to create the soup.

When the tomatoes have softened, start to add the chicken stock, just a ladle at a time, until you have a looser consistency. This brings us to personal choice. The soup can be as thick or as thin as you like. Leave it to cook for a further 20 minutes. Check for seasoning, and you may find that a little tomato purée will help the strength of taste. The soup is now ready to serve.

Cabbage Soup with Dumplings

Good food does not have to be made with fancy, unusual ingredients. Everyday produce will cook and taste just as delicious. This recipe is easy to prepare, simple to cook and cheap to make – and it can be served as a starter or a complete meal (see pp. 26–7). The dish itself came together purely by accident. I was braising some cabbage for one dish and making dumplings for a beef stew. The cabbage and dumplings became an instant success, as it has plenty of textures, tastes and flavours from just a few ingredients.

Both the cabbage soup and dumpling recipes are very basic and can, of course, be varied – a little garlic in the soup, or different herbs and spices in the dumplings. Even the Spinach Dumplings on page 150 could be rolled smaller and used as a garnish.

SERVES 4–6

1 Savoy cabbage, finely shredded
50 g (2 oz) unsalted butter
1.2 litres (2 pints) Chicken Stock (see
    p. 228) or Vegetable Stock (see p. 229)

2 onions, finely shredded
6 smoked bacon rashers, rinded and cut
    into thin strips
Salt and freshly ground white pepper

For the Dumplings

225 g (8 oz) plain flour
15 g (½ oz) baking powder
100 g (4 oz) dried shredded suet
½ teaspoon chopped fresh thyme
1 teaspoon chopped fresh basil

About 150 ml (5 fl oz) water
450 ml (15 fl oz) Chicken Stock (see
    p. 228) or Vegetable Stock (see
    p. 229), warmed

If you are baking the dumplings (see below), pre-heat the oven to 200°C/400°F/gas 6.

To make the dumplings, mix together the flour, baking powder, suet and herbs and season with salt and pepper. Gradually add just enough water until the mixture forms a dough. Leave to rest for 20 minutes then roll into 2 cm (¾ in) balls. These can be placed in the warm stock and either cooked in the pre-heated oven or on top of the stove, allowing them to bake or simmer slowly for about 20 minutes.

While the dumplings are cooking, cook the cabbage. Place the butter in a warm pan, add the onions and cook for 5 minutes without allowing them to colour. Add the bacon and cook for a further 5 minutes. Pour in the stock, bring to the simmer and simmer for 5–10 minutes. Bring to the boil, add the cabbage and simmer for about 4–5 minutes until tender. Check the seasoning and add the dumplings. The dish is now complete.

Ham and Vegetable Soup

To achieve the maximum taste from this soup it is best to buy some fresh ham or bacon, to soak it in cold water for 24 hours to remove any saltiness, and then cook it in some stock. This will create a good ham stock, and you can cut up the meat to go in the soup. If this all sounds a bit too much, then you can make a vegetable broth and I would suggest you add some diced smoked ham to give a more pronounced flavour. Anyway, here is my recipe for the original idea.

The soup can be served as a starter, main course or a supper dish. It looks lovely in a bowl with all the colours and tastes there. You can make it with your own favourite vegetables and serve it with garlic toasts and Parmesan, fried croûtons or just good old-fashioned bread and butter!

SERVES 8 as a starter,
4–6 as a supper or main course

For the Ham or Bacon

900 g (2 lb) raw bacon or ham collar, soaked in cold water for 24 hours
1 onion
2 carrots
1 leek
2 celery sticks
1 sprig of fresh thyme
1 bay leaf
25 g (1 oz) unsalted butter
2.25 litres (4 pints) Chicken Stock (see p. 228) or water

For the Soup

450 g (1 lb) carrots
2 onions
6 celery sticks
450 g (1 lb) swede
450 g (1 lb) parsnips
100 g (4 oz) unsalted butter
50 ml (2 fl oz) olive oil
1 large garlic clove, crushed
50 g (2 oz) pearl barley (optional)
Salt and freshly ground white pepper

To cook the ham or bacon, roughly chop all the vegetables into 1 cm (½ in) dice and cook in the butter for about 5 minutes without allowing them to colour. Add the herbs, cover and continue to cook until slightly softened. Keeping a lid on the vegetables will create steam within the pan; this prevents them from colouring and cooks them at the same time.

Pour on the chicken stock and bring to the simmer. Add the bacon or ham and bring back to the simmer. Cover the pan and cook for about 45 minutes. Leave the meat to stand in its own cooking liquor until cold. This part of the job can be done the day before or in the morning. It keeps the meat moist and helps the stock take on the maximum taste.

Remove the bacon or ham from the stock and cut it into 1 cm (½ in) cubes. Strain the stock through a sieve.

To prepare the soup, roughly chop all the vegetables into 1 cm (½ in) dice, keeping the swede and parsnip separate from the others. Melt the butter in a large pan with the olive oil. Add the carrots, onions, celery and garlic, cover and cook for 2–3 minutes. Add the pearl barley, if using, and cook for a further 2–3 minutes, stirring from time to time. Pour on the reserved stock and bring to the simmer. Allow the soup to simmer gently until the diced carrots are softened, about 20 minutes.

Add the diced swede and parsnips and continue to cook for a further 10 minutes until all the vegetables are cooked. Add the diced bacon or ham and season with salt and pepper.

66 *We've all heard of moules marinère, but this is my variation on how to eat mussels – it's nutty, garlicky and buttery.* **99**

Mussels with Garlic, Almonds and Parsley (see p. 37).

Mussel and Macaroni Soup

This soup is very wholesome, and I like to eat it as a supper dish with toasted French bread in the bowl – this soaks up all the juices and is lovely to eat.

SERVES 4

For the Mussels

450 g (1 lb) fresh mussels
225 g (8 oz) mixed vegetables (carrot,
    onion, celery and leek), cut into
    6 mm (¼ in) dice
1 sprig of fresh thyme
1 bay leaf

6 black peppercorns
1 star anise (optional)
50 g (2 oz) unsalted butter
300 ml (10 fl oz) dry white wine
1.2 litres (2 pints) Fish Stock (see p. 227)

For the Soup

2 carrots, cut into 6 mm (¼ in) dice
2 onions, cut into 6 mm (¼ in) dice
4 celery sticks, cut into 6 mm (¼ in) dice
1 garlic clove, crushed
50 ml (2 fl oz) olive oil
100 g (4 oz) unsalted butter
1 bouquet garni (1 bay leaf, 1 star anise,
    a few fresh basil leaves, 1 sprig each
    of fresh thyme and tarragon tied in

    a square of muslin) or bouquet garni
    sachet
300 ml (10 fl oz) dry white wine
100 g (4 oz) dried or fresh macaroni,
    cooked
6 tomatoes, skinned, seeded and diced
1½ tablespoons Pesto Sauce (see p. 243)
A few knobs of unsalted butter
Salt and freshly ground white pepper

Scrape and wash the mussels well. Remove the beards (the threads that hang out of the shells). Discard any mussels that gape and do not close when tapped sharply with a knife.

To cook the mussels, sweat all the diced vegetables, herbs and spices in the butter for a few minutes, then add the white wine and boil to reduce until almost dry. Add the fish stock, bring to the simmer and cook for 10 minutes. Bring the liquor to the boil and add the mussels. Cover with a lid and shake carefully. The mussels will start to open after a few minutes. Drain the mussels and pass the stock through a fine sieve. Discard the vegetables and spices. Remove the mussels from their shells and keep them moist in a little of the stock. Discard any that have remained closed.

To make the soup, sweat the diced vegetables and garlic in the olive oil and butter for a few minutes. Add the bouquet garni and continue to cook for about 4–5 minutes until the vegetables have softened. Add the white wine and boil to reduce until almost dry. Pour in the mussel stock and simmer for 15–20 minutes.

To finish the soup, add the cooked macaroni, tomatoes and shelled mussels. Stir in the pesto sauce and a few knobs of butter, remove the bouquet garni and taste for seasoning before serving.

Mussels with Garlic, Almonds and Parsley

This is usually served as a starter, but it also makes a great main course (see p. 34).

SERVES 4

For the Butter

6 shallots, finely chopped
1 large garlic clove, crushed

250 g (9 oz) unsalted butter, softened

For the Mussel Cooking Liquor

½ onion, chopped
1 carrot, chopped
2 celery sticks, chopped
1 small leek, chopped
15 g (½ oz) unsalted butter
1 garlic clove, crushed
1 bay leaf

1 sprig of fresh thyme
½ bottle dry white wine
600 ml (1 pint) Fish Stock
(see p. 227)
1 kg (2¼ lb) mussels, scrubbed
and bearded (see previous recipe)

For the Garnish

50 g (2 oz) nibbed almonds, lightly
toasted
2 tablespoons chopped fresh parsley

4 slices white bread, crusts removed,
crumbed and toasted until
golden

Sweat the chopped shallots and garlic in 1 tablespoon of the butter until translucent, then leave to cool. Mix them with most of the remaining butter and keep aside for later.

To start the mussel liquor, sweat the chopped onion, carrot, celery and leek in the butter with the garlic, bay leaf and thyme for a few minutes. Add the white wine and boil to reduce until almost dry. Add the fish stock and bring to the boil, then add the mussels. Stir until the shells begin to open, then remove from the heat.

Strain the cooking liquor through a fine sieve and discard the vegetables. Remove the mussels from their shells, discarding any that have not opened, and remove any sinews from the mussels. Keep them moist in a little of the stock. Rinse the shells.

Boil the liquor to reduce it until a good mussel flavour is achieved, then gradually add the shallot and garlic butter in knobs. Add the mussels, toasted almonds and parsley. Place some of the shells in a circle on large individual bowls or plates. Spoon the mussels into the shells and pour over some of the cooking liquor. To finish the dish, sprinkle with the warm, golden toasted breadcrumbs.

Red Mullet Soup

I love all fish soups, but I find red mullet gives the best taste. For this soup, fresh or frozen red mullet fillets can be used. Garlic toasts with Rouille (see p. 241) are delicious with this soup. Cut a French stick into 1 cm (½ in) slices and spread with some garlic butter (simply mix crushed garlic to taste into softened butter). Toast the slices then top with Rouille.

SERVES 8–10

225 g (8 oz) tomatoes, chopped
1 fennel bulb, chopped
1 large onion, chopped
2 carrots, chopped
1 leek, chopped
2 celery sticks, chopped
1 garlic clove, crushed
½ bunch of fresh basil
½ bunch of fresh tarragon
A pinch of saffron

25 ml (1 fl oz) olive oil
50 g (2 oz) unsalted butter
450 g (1 lb) red mullet fillets, scaled and sliced into pieces
300 ml (10 fl oz) Noilly Prat or dry white vermouth
300 ml (10 fl oz) dry white wine
1.2 litres (2 pints) Fish Stock (see p. 227)
2 teaspoons tomato purée
Salt and freshly ground white pepper

Sweat all the chopped vegetables, garlic, herbs and saffron in the olive oil and butter for a few minutes. Add the red mullet fillets, the Noilly Prat and white wine and allow to cook and reduce for 5–6 minutes. Pour on the fish stock and tomato purée. Bring the soup to the simmer and cook for 40 minutes.

Purée the soup in a food processor or liquidizer and push through a sieve. Season with salt and pepper. The soup should be a rich, orangey-red colour with a powerful depth of flavour and eats beautifully with the Rouille toasts (see p. 241 and above).

Cod Brandade
with Warm Poached Egg

This dish needs a lot of planning and thinking time, but really is worth every effort. The basic mixture makes more than you need for four, because 75 g (3 oz) will be enough per starter portion. The rest of the mixture can be stored in the fridge for a day or so and can be rolled into balls and coated with breadcrumbs then deep-fried as for the Salmon Fish Cakes (see p. 88).

SERVES 4

900 g (2 lb) cod fillet with skin	1 large garlic clove, finely chopped
Rock salt	1–1.5 kg (2–3 lb) Mashed Potatoes
8 black peppercorns	without cream or butter
1 sprig of fresh thyme	(see p. 142)
1 bay leaf	2 tablespoons chopped fresh parsley
200 ml (7 fl oz) olive oil	Freshly ground white pepper

To serve

Milk	300 ml (10 fl oz) Brandade Dressing
4 eggs, poached	(see p. 40)
(see p. 56)	Olive oil

Sprinkle the cod liberally with rock salt, cover and place in the fridge for 48 hours, turning it at least once. After the fish has been salted, it needs to be washed to remove the salt, then soaked for 12 hours in cold water.

Drain the fish well and cut it into eight pieces. Place in a pan with the peppercorns, thyme and bay leaf and just cover with cold water. Bring to the boil then remove from the heat and allow to cool. Remove the cod from the liquid, take off the skin and pick out any bones. Flake the flesh.

Warm the olive oil in a large pan then add the cod. While it is cooking for a few minutes, add the garlic and break up the fish with a wooden spoon. Add some mashed potatoes, working on a ratio of two parts potato to one part cod. Add the parsley and season with white pepper. This mixture can now be left to cool, then chilled.

To serve the brandade, place it in a pan with a little milk over a gentle heat until warmed through. While the cod is warming, poach the eggs. Then spoon the cod on to the centre of the plates and sit the warm poached eggs on top. Spoon the dressing generously all around and trickle a little extra olive oil over the eggs.

Brandade Dressing

This may look fairly complex, but in fact is very simple to make. This recipe will make a reasonable amount and will keep very well in the fridge. It's also absolutely delicious to eat with the Cod Brandade or other salads.

MAKES about 600 ml (1 pint)

1 onion, finely chopped
½ teaspoon chopped fresh thyme
½ teaspoon chopped fresh rosemary
½ teaspoon chopped fresh basil
½ teaspoon chopped fresh parsley
1 garlic clove, crushed
50 g (2 oz) unsalted butter
500 ml (17 fl oz) olive oil
300 ml (10 fl oz) red wine
50 g (2 oz) shelled walnuts, chopped

50 g (2 oz) black olives, stoned and chopped
25 g (1 oz) anchovy fillets, drained and chopped
25 g (1 oz) capers, drained and chopped
1 fennel bulb, cooked (see p. 84), and cut into 6 mm (¼ in) dice
8 tomatoes, skinned, seeded and diced
Salt and freshly ground white pepper

In a large pan, sweat the chopped onion, herbs and garlic in the butter and 3 tablespoons of olive oil for a few minutes. Add the red wine and boil to reduce until almost dry. Add the remaining olive oil and all the remaining ingredients except the tomatoes, bring to the simmer and simmer for a few minutes. Add the diced tomatoes, season with salt and pepper and remove from the heat. The sauce is now ready.

Soused Mackerel
with Warm Potatoes

Sousing or pickling is usually associated with raw fish. This recipe is slightly different. The mackerel is heated briefly in its spicy liquor, then served warm with the potatoes. This makes the liquor a sauce, and the addition of potato makes the mackerel a complete dish (see overleaf).

Serves 4

1 small fennel bulb, very thinly sliced
2 carrots, thinly sliced
2 celery sticks, thinly sliced
1 leek, thinly sliced
2 shallots or 1 onion, thinly sliced
1 bouquet garni (1 bay leaf, 1 star anise, a few fresh basil leaves, 2 sprigs each of fresh thyme and tarragon tied in a square of muslin or a strip of leek leaves) or bouquet garni sachet

6 black peppercorns
50 ml (2 fl oz) olive oil
100 g (4 oz) unsalted butter
150 ml (5 fl oz) dry white wine
150 ml (5 fl oz) white wine vinegar
600 ml (1 pint) water
4 mackerel fillets, all bones removed
Salt and freshly ground white pepper
1 quantity Mashed Potatoes with lemon and shallots (see p. 142)
1 tablespoon chopped fresh parsley

Cook all the sliced vegetables in a pan with the bouquet garni, peppercorns, olive oil and half the butter for a few minutes. Add the white wine, wine vinegar and water and simmer for about 10–12 minutes until the vegetables are cooked. This is your sousing liquor. Allow to cool and remove the bouquet garni.

Place the fillets in a lightly buttered flameproof dish and cover with the liquor and vegetables. Season with salt and pepper. Bring slowly to the simmer then remove from the heat. The fish is now ready.

Spoon some of the hot mashed potatoes into serving bowls and sit the mackerel on top. Stir the remaining butter and the parsley into the cooking liquor. Spoon the vegetables and sauce around the fish and serve.

*Soused Mackerel
with Warm Potatoes
(see p. 41).*

Grilled Mackerel
with Stewed Tomatoes, Pesto
and Onions

Here we are looking at simple ingredients, and we all know that tomatoes, onions, garlic and basil work well together (see pp. 222–3). I have added the slight Italian influence, using pesto sauce. This has so many uses: as a seasoning, a sauce on its own, or to flavour cream sauces or tomatoes. It can be made at home, but good pesto can be found in almost any supermarket or delicatessen.

I use the mackerel as a starter and so only serve one fillet a portion, but like most dishes this would also make a good main course for two.

Serves 4

For the Tomatoes, Pesto and Onions

2–3 tablespoons olive oil	12 tomatoes, preferably plum, skinned
3 onions, thinly sliced	and quartered
	1 tablespoon Pesto Sauce (see p. 243)

For the Mackerel

Salt and freshly ground white pepper	1 tablespoon plain flour
Oil for deep-frying (preferably	Curly endive leaves
ground-nut)	1–2 tablespoons Basic Vinaigrette
25 g (1 oz) unsalted butter	(see p. 245)
4 mackerel fillets, all bones removed	

Pour the olive oil into a pan and add one-third of the sliced onions. Allow to cook gently for about 10 minutes until the onions are soft but not coloured. Add the quartered tomatoes and continue to cook for 15–20 minutes until the tomatoes have stewed with the onions, creating their own sauce. Add the pesto sauce to taste (approximately a tablespoon will be enough) and season with salt and pepper.

Pre-heat the grill to moderate and heat the oil for deep-frying. Brush a tray with a little of the butter and season it with salt and pepper. Lay the mackerel fillets on top and brush with butter. Cook the fillets under the grill for about 5–6 minutes until the skin is crisp. Meanwhile, lightly dust the remaining onions with flour. Fry in the deep hot fat until golden and crisp. Drain well and season with a little salt.

Spoon some of the warm tomato mixture on to individual plates. Dress the curly endive with a little vinaigrette and place a few leaves on to each tomato mound. Lay the mackerel fillets on top and finish the dish with the crispy onions.

Grilled Sardine Fillets
on Tomato Toasts

This is a similar dish to the mackerel recipe (p. 44) but with this we've created different tastes and textures. It's not just an alternative, therefore, but a dish quite rightly out on its own (see pp. 234–5). It may sound a little complicated but believe me, it's simple and tasty, so try it!

SERVES 4

8 fresh sardines, scaled and filleted
4 tablespoons olive oil
Juice of ½ lemon
Salt and freshly ground white pepper
4 × 1 cm (½ in) slices crusty or onion
    bread
1 quantity Stewed Tomatoes, Pesto and
    Onions (see p. 44)
300 ml (10 fl oz) Hollandaise Sauce (see
    p. 244) (optional)

In a dish large enough to hold the sardines in one layer, mix the olive oil with the lemon juice and season with salt and pepper. Lay the sardine fillets into the oil and leave for 1–2 hours to take on the taste.

Brush the bread slices with a little of the marinade oil. These slices can now be toasted on both sides until golden. Warm the stewed tomatoes with pesto.

Pre-heat the grill to hot. Season the sardine fillets with salt and pepper and lay them on a tray or grill rack and place under the hot grill. Just cook until slightly coloured. Providing the grill is hot this will only take 2–3 minutes.

To serve, spoon some hollandaise sauce, if using, on to four plates or into bowls, spreading it a little into a circle. Sit the toasts on top, and spoon the tomatoes with pesto on to them. Sit the sardines overlapping on top and just pour a little of the excess oil from the tray over the fish.

Smoked Eel Kedgeree

This dish could also be called a smoked eel risotto because it's made by the risotto method, but it holds all the flavours of a good old-fashioned kedgeree. I serve it as a starter, but it can be a total meal in itself. Hard-boiled eggs are traditionally used, but having a warm poached egg sitting on top of the rice and just breaking the yolk over it is a dream. The recipe for the Curry Cream Sauce is on page 237, but you can buy a ready-made one just to make the dish a little easier. If you really cannot find smoked eel, you can make the dish with smoked haddock.

SERVES 4

900 g (2 lb) smoked eel

For the Eel Stock

1 onion, chopped
1 leek, chopped
2 celery sticks, chopped
6 mushrooms or 50 g (2 oz) mushroom
    trimmings
1 bay leaf
1 sprig of fresh thyme

2 sprigs of fresh tarragon
A few black peppercorns
50 g (2 oz) unsalted butter
300 ml (10 fl oz) dry white wine
1.2 litres (2 pints) Fish Stock (see p. 227)
    or water

For the Kedgeree

2 onions, finely chopped
100 g (4 oz) unsalted butter
50 g (2 oz) bone marrow, chopped
    (optional)

1 garlic clove, crushed
225 g (8 oz) arborio or long-grain rice
½ quantity Curry Cream Sauce
    (see p. 237)

To serve

4 eggs, poached (see p. 66)
3 tablespoons olive oil
2 teaspoons snipped fresh chives

Smoked eel is one of my favourite smoked fish. Firstly it has to be filleted and skinned. Hopefully your fishmonger will do this for you, but if not, simply cut off the head and position the knife against the top half of the central bone. Carefully cut along the bone, removing the fillet of fish. Turn the fish over and repeat the same process. Now the skin can be removed: slide your finger or thumb under the skin at the head end and it should tear off all the way along. The fillets may need a little trimming down the sides to remove any excess skin. Turn the fillets on to their back to show the centre. From the head end to half-way down there will be some bones. Simply position the knife under these bones, and cut away from the flesh. You now have two long, clean fillets of eel. Cut these into 2.5 cm (1 in) pieces and put in the fridge.

To make the eel stock, chop all the bones, skin and trimmings. Place the chopped vegetables, herbs and peppercorns in a large, warmed pan with the butter and cook them gently for 10 minutes without letting them colour. Add the bones and trimmings and continue to cook for a further 5 minutes. Add the white wine and boil to reduce until almost dry. Add the fish stock or water. (Fish stock will give you a stronger and better taste. If you are using water, ask the fishmonger to give you some fish bones as well to cook with the eel.) Bring the stock to the simmer and cook for 20 minutes. Strain through a sieve and the stock is ready.

For the kedgeree, cook the chopped onions in the butter with the bone marrow, if using, and the garlic for 5–6 minutes until softened. Stir in the rice and cook for 2 minutes, then start to add the hot eel stock a few tablespoons at a time, stirring continuously. This will create a steam and help the cooking process. Wait for the stock to be absorbed before adding more, and keep adding the stock and stirring until the rice is just softening – this will take about 15–20 minutes. The rice should be tender and the mixture still moist.

When the rice is cooked, stir in half the curry sauce and taste. At this stage it becomes a matter of personal choice; some more or all of the curry sauce can be added if you want a stronger taste.

Add the pieces of chopped eel to the kedgeree and stir in to warm through. Warm the poached eggs for a few minutes in a bowl of boiling water, then drain well. Spoon the kedgeree into four bowls and sit a poached egg on top of each one. Spoon a little olive oil over the eggs and sprinkle with the snipped chives. The dish is now ready.

Welsh Rarebit

This recipe is really the minimum amount you can make for a successful mixture. It will keep in the fridge for up to ten days, so can be used in plenty of other dishes. My favourite use is with the Smoked Haddock with tomato salad opposite. It's also delicious as a simple cheese on toast.

SERVES 16

700 g (1½ lb) mature Cheddar, grated
150 ml (5 fl oz) milk
25 g (1 oz) plain flour
50 g (2 oz) fresh white breadcrumbs
1 tablespoon English mustard powder
2 shakes of Worcestershire sauce
Salt and freshly ground white pepper
2 eggs
2 egg yolks

Put the Cheddar into a pan and add the milk. Slowly melt them together over a low heat, but do not allow the mix to boil as this will separate the cheese. When the mixture is smooth and just begins to bubble, add the flour, breadcrumbs and mustard and cook for a few minutes, stirring, over a low heat until the mixture comes away from the sides of the pan and begins to form a ball shape. Add the Worcestershire sauce, salt and pepper and leave to cool.

When cold, place the mixture into a food processor, turn on the motor and slowly add the eggs and egg yolks. (If you don't have a processor or mixer, just beat vigorously with a wooden spoon.) When the eggs are mixed in, chill for a few hours before using. After it has rested in the fridge, you will find the rarebit is very easy to handle and has so many uses. The mix also freezes very well. When I make it at home, I divide it into four and freeze three batches for use later!

Smoked Haddock
with Welsh Rarebit

This has to be one of my favourites – possibly a signature dish, and hopefully a classic (see overleaf). It's lovely as a starter or main course. Cheese and tomato are a great combination, so placing the haddock on to a tomato salad works really well and, of course, gives us those hot and cold tastes. Choose really good tomatoes – plum are much the best.

I have chosen natural smoked haddock which is quite white in colour. The yellow-dyed haddock is not really needed as the cheese is, of course, already that colour – and you know that I like natural tastes, textures and colours!

SERVES 4

6 ripe plum or salad tomatoes
Salt and freshly ground white pepper
4 × 100 g (4 oz) slices natural smoked
    haddock
175 g (6 oz) Welsh Rarebit mix (see left)
1 tablespoon finely snipped fresh chives
150 ml (5 fl oz) Basic Vinaigrette
    (see p. 245)

Pre-heat the oven to 180°C/350°F/gas 4 and pre-heat the grill to medium.

Firstly remove and discard the eyes from the tomatoes. Blanch the tomatoes in boiling water for 5–6 seconds. Cool them quickly in iced water and the skins should peel off easily. Slice the tomatoes and arrange overlapping on to the centre of individual plates. You'll need about 1½ tomatoes per portion, and this should make a nice circle. Sprinkle with a little salt and a twist of pepper.

Arrange the haddock portions in a buttered flameproof dish. Split the rarebit into four pieces, pat out on your hands to about 2–3 mm (⅛ in) thick and lay on top of the haddock (the mix should be quite pliable and easy to use). Colour under the grill until golden then finish the haddock in the pre-heated oven for 3–4 minutes.

Add the chives to the vinaigrette and spoon over the tomatoes. When the haddock is cooked, just sit on top of the tomatoes and serve.

Smoked Haddock with
Welsh Rarebit served on
a tomato salad
(see p. 49)

Ricotta and Spinach Gnocchi

Gnocchi is an Italian dish of little dumplings which can be made in three ways: with semolina, potato or flour and eggs. I'm using the latter with ricotta cheese, which is readily available and is probably the cheese most used in cooking in Italy.

Serves 4

350 g (12 oz) fresh spinach, stalks removed

175 g (6 oz) ricotta, drained and diced

1 egg

50 g (2 oz) plain flour

25 g (1 oz) Parmesan, grated

A pinch of freshly grated nutmeg

Salt and freshly ground white pepper

For the Dressing

150 ml (5 fl oz) olive oil

4 shallots or 1 large onion, finely chopped

1 large garlic clove, crushed

6 tomatoes, skinned, seeded and chopped

Juice of ½ lemon

1 bunch of fresh basil, chopped

To serve

Parmesan flakes

Wash the spinach well to remove any grit then shake off any excess water. Place the spinach into a hot pan and cook in its own water for a few minutes until the leaves begin to wilt. Remove them from the pan and squeeze out any excess liquid. Blitz the spinach in a food processor or chop it very finely. Mix the spinach with the ricotta, egg, flour and Parmesan and season with nutmeg, salt and pepper. Leave the mixture to rest in the fridge for 20 minutes.

To make the dressing, warm the olive oil with the chopped shallots or onion and garlic and cook over a gentle heat for about 15 minutes. Add the chopped tomatoes and continue to cook for a further 5 minutes. Season with salt and pepper and add the lemon juice. Keep the dressing warm while you cook the gnocchi.

Using floured hands, shape the gnocchi into small 2.5 cm (1 in) balls. Bring a large pan of salted water to the boil (or you could use vegetable stock) and drop the gnocchi into the boiling water. When the balls rise to the surface after just a few minutes they are cooked. Remove them from the pan using a slotted spoon and drain well. Add the chopped basil to the dressing at the last minute, just before serving, then roll the gnocchi in the dressing and divide between four bowls. Sprinkle with some Parmesan flakes and serve.

*Ricotta and Spinach Gnocchi
with a tomato and basil
dressing.*

Poached Egg Salad
with Sauté Potatoes, Black Pudding
and Bacon

I have always wanted to do something with the Great British Breakfast, it has so many potential combinations. Here is an idea that acts as a starter for lunch, dinner or a complete meal on its own. The leaves listed below are good for this salad as they have different tastes and colours, but you can use any lettuces available to you. The most exciting part of eating this dish is breaking into the egg yolk and mixing it with the salad and sauce. It's tasty, rich and a delight to eat (see pp. 58–9).

SERVES 4

1 tablespoon white wine or malt vinegar (using white wine vinegar prevents any discolouration)

4 eggs

225 g (8 oz) new potatoes, boiled and sliced

50 g (2 oz) unsalted butter

175 g (6 oz) smoked bacon, rinded and cut into strips

½ black pudding, cut into 1 cm (½ in) pieces

A few lettuce leaves per person (lollo rosso, oak leaf, curly endive, rocket)

150 ml (5 fl oz) Basic Vinaigrette (see p. 245)

150 ml (5 fl oz) Red Wine Sauce (see p. 236) (optional)

Salt and freshly ground white pepper

Bring a large, deep pan of water to a rolling boil, add the wine vinegar, then crack the eggs into the water. Poach for about 4 minutes until the white has set. Remove from the pan with a slotted spoon and place in a bowl of cold water.

Fry the potato slices in the butter until golden and crisp on both sides. Remove from the pan and keep warm. Fry the bacon until crisp and nicely browned. Add to the potatoes. Fry the black pudding for a few minutes on both sides and keep warm with the bacon and potatoes.

Separate the lettuce leaves carefully and wash in a little salted water. Drain and shake off any excess water. Place in a bowl and dress with most of the vinaigrette.

The finishing of the salad is up to you. I like to almost 'build' my salad by firstly placing some potatoes, black pudding and bacon on to the plates or bowls and then the lettuce leaves followed by more potatoes etc. until I have what you might call a designer salad, but still looking quite natural. The simplest way is just to mix your garnishes with the salad leaves and separate on to plates.

While assembling the salad, warm the red wine sauce, if using, and re-heat the poached eggs for 1–2 minutes in a bowl of hot water. Drain the eggs well, place on top of the salad and sprinkle with a little of the remaining vinaigrette and a twist of pepper. Pour the red wine sauce around and serve.

Poached Egg Salad
with Sauté Potatoes,
Black Pudding and Bacon
(see p. 56).

Spanish Omelette

This must be one of the cheapest dishes to produce, and also one of the simplest to make. A Spanish friend of mine gave me this recipe and it works every time. Most tapas bars serve Spanish omelettes, but I've yet to have one as good as this. It can be served as a starter, snack or main course, and I like to serve it with the Red Pepper and Anchovy Salad which follows.

Serves 4

2 large potatoes, thinly sliced	4 eggs, beaten
1 onion, sliced	1 teaspoon olive oil
Salt and freshly ground white pepper	1 quantity Red Pepper and Anchovy
Ground-nut or vegetable oil for	Salad (see opposite)
deep-frying	A handful of salad leaves

Mix the potatoes with the sliced onions and sprinkle them lightly with salt. Heat the ground-nut oil to about 140–150°C (285–300°F) and blanch the potatoes and onions in batches in a deep-fat fryer for about 4–5 minutes, making sure you cook them without colouring. Make sure the oil is not too hot, and while the potatoes are blanching, turn them with a fork to ensure even cooking. When cooked, drain off all excess oil. Mix the potatoes, onions and eggs and season with salt and pepper.

Heat a 15 cm (6 in) frying-pan with sloping sides and trickle in the olive oil. Pour in the potato and egg mixture and move with the fork as the first side is cooking. It should take a few minutes until it is golden brown. Turn the omelette on to a plate then slide it back into the pan to cook the other side. Leave to rest, as it is best eaten just warm. Serve in wedges with a little of the red pepper and anchovy salad, on plates garnished with salad leaves.

Red Pepper and Anchovy Salad

The only way to serve this is to use the marinated and oiled anchovy fillets. These can be obtained from a delicatessen, usually sold loose over the counter. If the only ones available are tinned, then it would be best just to serve a red pepper salad.

SERVES 4–6

2 red peppers
12 anchovy fillets (not tinned)
2–3 tablespoons Vierge Dressing
(see p. 249)

Pre-heat the grill to hot. Put the whole red peppers under the hot grill and wait until the skin begins to colour and bubble. Turn the pepper until this has happened all round. While the peppers are still warm, peel off all the skin and leave to cool. When cold, halve the peppers and remove all the seeds. Cut the peppers into thin strips and cover with vierge dressing. It is now best to leave them for 1–2 hours to marinate.

Just before serving, split the anchovy fillets in half lengthways and mix them with the peppers. Serve with the Spanish omelette.

Chicken Liver Parfait

This is a great dish for a starter or a main item on a cold buffet (see pp. 222–3). I like to serve a slice on a plate with some good, thick toast, a few lettuce leaves and home-made Grape Chutney (see p. 251) or Green Tomato Chutney (see p. 251). I always cook this parfait in a loaf tin or porcelain terrine mould, but of course individual 7.5 cm (3 in) moulds can be used.

SERVES 8–10

For the Parfait

750 g (1½ lb) chicken livers, soaked for at least 24 hours in cold milk
1 garlic clove, crushed
Pinch of freshly grated nutmeg
Salt and freshly ground white pepper
3 eggs

900 ml (1½ pints) double cream
3 tablespoons brandy
About 3 tablespoons Veal *Jus* (see p. 232) or bought alternative (see p. 225) (optional)

Pre-heat the oven to 160°C/325°F/gas 3. Butter a 30 × 8 × 8 cm (12 × 3 × 3 in) terrine dish with a lid, a 900 g (2 lb) loaf tin, or eight to ten 7.5 cm (3 in) ramekin dishes and line them all with greaseproof paper.

Soaking the livers in milk removes any bitter taste. Drain the milk from the livers and discard the milk. For the best results with this recipe you will need a food processor or liquidizer. Blitz the livers in the processor with the garlic, nutmeg, salt and pepper until smooth. Add the eggs and blitz for a further 1 minute. Add the cream, brandy and *jus,* if using. (The *jus* is optional for this recipe, but I find it gives a little depth and flavour to the parfait.) Continue to blitz for a few seconds and then check for seasoning. The parfait should now be pushed through a fine sieve to give a smoother consistency. You will now find the mix to be quite liquid.

Pour the mix into the prepared terrine or moulds and cover with a lid. Stand in a tray filled with warm water to come half-way up the sides of the terrine to ensure a slow, steady cooking, and cook in the pre-heated oven for about 1½ hours. Make sure the parfait is checked after 30 minutes and 1 hour. After 1 hour, check every 10 minutes until the parfait is just firming to the touch. It will, of course, continue to cook once removed from the oven until it has completely cooled. Remove from the water bath and leave to cool then chill for 2–3 hours.

To serve the parfait, dip the mould into hot water and turn it over on to a chopping board. Remove the greaseproof paper and slice as needed. The parfait can be wrapped in cling film and kept in the fridge for 2–3 days.

Grilled Ham, Cheese and Tomato Toasts

This recipe is a designer sandwich which I often make from left-overs or as a complete supper meal. The cooked ham I'm using here is from my Boiled Bacon recipe (see p. 113) – there always seems to be some left over. Of course, you don't have to cook bacon or ham just for this recipe; I'm sure you can buy some good cooked ham at the shops. Welsh rarebit, however, is a must for this dish. Plain melted cheese just isn't the same.

SERVES 4

4 slices crusty bread
50 g (2 oz) unsalted butter
4 slices cooked bacon or ham (see above)
4 plum or salad tomatoes, sliced
Freshly ground black pepper
175 g (6 oz) Welsh Rarebit mix (see p. 48)
4 eggs, poached (see p. 56)
1 teaspoon chopped fresh parsley
50 ml (2 fl oz) Basic Vinaigrette
    (see p. 245)

Pre-heat the grill to hot. Butter the slices of bread and toast them on both sides. Lay the ham on to the buttered side. Cover with the sliced tomatoes and season with pepper. Split the rarebit into four pieces, pat out on your hands to the size and shape of the toast and lay on top of the tomatoes. Sit the toasts under the hot grill and colour the rarebit mix golden brown.

Warm the poached eggs for a few minutes in a bowl of boiling water. Put the toasts on individual plates and top each one with a poached egg. Mix the chopped parsley with the vinaigrette and spoon over the top.

The Rhodes 'Open' Club Sandwich

A club sandwich was one of the first dishes that I ever had to make – this was at the Amsterdam Hilton. The coffee shop was always packed, and the club sandwich was one of its most popular choices. This is my version and I hope you enjoy it (see p. 27). It's having just one slice of toast that makes this 'Open'. Make it as a starter for dinner parties – nobody will expect to be served a sandwich!

Makes 2 sandwiches

2 slices bread of your choice
soft butter
1 chicken breast, skinned
Salt and freshly ground white pepper
1 tablespoon olive oil (if necessary)
2 rashers smoked or green back bacon,
    rinded
½ iceberg lettuce, shredded

1 tablespoon finely chopped onion
2 tablespoons Mayonnaise
    (see p. 248)
2–3 tomatoes, thinly sliced
2 tablespoons Basic Vinaigrette
    (see p. 245)
1 teaspoon chopped fresh parsley
2 poached eggs, warmed (see p. 56)

Pre-heat the grill to hot. Butter the bread on both sides and then toast it under the grill until golden brown.

Split the chicken breast lengthways through the middle and season with salt and pepper. Grill, or pan-fry in the olive oil, for a few minutes on each side until cooked. Grill the bacon until crisp. Mix the shredded lettuce and onion with the mayonnaise and season with salt and pepper.

Lay the tomato slices on top of the two pieces of toast and sprinkle with some of the vinaigrette. Divide the lettuce mixture between the two and top with the bacon and chicken breast halves. Sit the warmed poached eggs on the chicken breasts and mix the chopped parsley with the remaining vinaigrette and sprinkle over them.

Beef Carpaccio

This dish originated in the 1950s and was named after the Italian painter, Vittore Carpaccio, known for the reds and whites in his work. It has now become a favourite starter across the world. Here is my version (see p. 67).

SERVES at least 8

900 g (2 lb) topside of beef
50 g (2 oz) Parmesan
Freshly ground black pepper

For the Marinade

150 ml (5 fl oz) balsamic vinegar
5 tablespoons soy sauce
5 tablespoons Worcestershire sauce
4 garlic cloves, chopped
1 bunch of fresh basil

½ bunch of fresh thyme
15 black peppercorns, crushed
300 ml (10 fl oz) dry white wine
600 ml (1 pint) olive oil
15 g (½ oz) coarse sea salt

Trim the beef of any fat and sinew, which will leave you with 750–800 g (1½–1¾ lb) of meat.

Mix together all the marinade ingredients, reserving a few basil leaves to finish the dish. Roll the beef in the marinade, cover and leave to steep in the fridge for 4–5 days to achieve the maximum taste. The beef should be turned in the marinade every day. If the beef is kept in the oil in the fridge, you could leave it for up to 10–12 days.

After the marinating process, remove the meat from the marinade and wrap in cling film. Freeze it, if you like, to use later, or it can even be sliced from frozen on a slicing machine. It can also be kept in the fridge and sliced very thinly with a sharp knife as you want it. Push the marinade through a sieve to use as the dressing.

To serve the carpaccio, slice it very thinly and place the slices on to the serving plate, covering the whole surface (about three to four slices if cut by hand, four to five if cut on a machine). Chop the remaining basil leaves and add to the dressing. Brush this over the meat and twist on some freshly ground black pepper. The Parmesan can be sliced from a piece into shavings and laid on top, or it can be grated and served separately.

66 I don't stop at British dishes. A lot of my favourites are Italian and French, and most of them are just too good to ignore. 99

Beef Carpaccio with shavings of Parmesan cheese (see p. 65).

Breast of Pigeon Wrapped in Cabbage on a Warm Potato Salad

Try to find squab pigeons to make this dish. These are specially reared young pigeons, and are very tender and plump. By doubling the quantities this could also be served as a main course. As a variation, a pigeon red wine sauce can be made by adding the pigeon carcasses to the reduction of the Red Wine Sauce (see p. 236) and then continuing with the recipe. The legs and carcass will infuse the sauce, giving it a rich, gamey flavour.

SERVES 4

2 squab pigeons
225 g (8 oz) mushrooms, minced or finely chopped
2 chicken livers, chopped
4 chicken hearts (optional), chopped
50 g (2 oz) wild mushrooms (optional), chopped

Salt and freshly ground black pepper
1 egg yolk
4 large green cabbage leaves
100 g (4 oz) pig's caul, soaked in cold water for 24 hours (optional)
50 g (2 oz) unsalted butter

For the Warm Potato Salad

450 g (1 lb) new potatoes, cooked
2 tablespoons olive oil
300 ml (10 fl oz) Red Wine Vinaigrette (see p. 248)

½ teaspoon chopped fresh parsley
½ teaspoon chopped fresh tarragon
½ teaspoon snipped fresh chives

Remove the legs and breasts from the carcasses. Skin the breasts but keep them whole. Cut up all the meat on the legs.

Place the minced or chopped mushrooms in a pan and cook over a low heat until almost dry. Allow to cool. Mix in the chopped leg meat, and the chopped chicken livers, hearts and wild mushrooms, if using. Season with salt and pepper and bind with the egg yolk.

Blanch the cabbage leaves quickly in boiling salted water then refresh in cold water and dry on a cloth. Lay them flat and sit the pigeon breasts on top of each one. Spread about 5 mm (¼ in) of the minced filling on top of each breast and fold over the cabbage until you have a small cabbage parcel. Cut the pig's caul into four and wrap a piece around each cabbage parcel. The parcels are now ready.

Heat the butter in a frying-pan and cook the pigeon parcels for about 5–6 minutes on each side until golden brown.

While the cooked potatoes for the salad are still warm, peel and slice them and mix with the olive oil, then season with salt and pepper. Keep them warm. Mix the red wine vinaigrette with the chopped herbs. Divide the potatoes between four plates and spoon the dressing over each portion. Make two or three cuts through the breasts, arrange them on top of the potatoes and serve.

Main Courses

It is in these main course recipes that you will find some of my favourite Great British Classics (although there are, admittedly, quite a few in the pudding section, too). They're arranged in various categories – fish, meat and poultry, and vegetarian and vegetable dishes – which will, I hope, help you find more easily what you're looking for.

ABOVE *Cod with a Parsley Crust (see p. 74) served on Mashed Potatoes (see p. 142) with Lemon Butter Sauce (see p. 243).*
LEFT *Jambonette de Volaille (see p. 96) served with Ratatouille Sauce (see p. 76) or Braised Butter Beans (see p. 99).*

Fish

Most chefs seem to prefer cooking fish to meat, but whether that's because it cooks so quickly or because it is so adaptable and versatile, I'm not quite sure. Most of the fish used here are easily available from good fishmongers or fish counters in supermarkets, but if you can't find, say, skate or tuna, you can always substitute with something similar.

When buying fish, there are some obvious signs that will alert you as to its freshness. Most fresh flat fish have what is almost a wet slime over their skins. All fish should have bright, rounded (*not* sunken) eyes, and the flesh should be firm to the touch. Some older fish, or fish that have been frozen, have flesh that is full of water, so soft that it almost falls apart.

I love using fresh cod, mostly from British waters, which has a firm, white and very meaty flesh. Some of the best sea bass, turbot and red mullet comes from Brixham in the West Country. And Scotland, of course, is the origin of some of the best smoked fish, particularly haddock and salmon. Herrings are another Scottish speciality and there's plenty more where all these came from.

Cod with a Parsley Crust was one of my first fish dishes. The nicest thing about it is all the different textures – the crisp breadcrumb topping, the flesh of the fish, and then the creamy mashed potatoes. The whole thing is finished with a light lemon sauce. Salmon Fish Cakes are another old favourite. I took them off the menu at the Greenhouse for a little while, but had to restore them after a lot of harassment from customers – they had to make a return visit. If you can't get salmon – or think it's too expensive for a fish cake – then use cod instead; the recipe works just as well.

One of the dishes that has travelled with me is the Steamed Fillet of Turbot on Green Vegetables. The flavours of ginger and lime work so well together, and act almost as a seasoning for the vegetables. If you want to go even more oriental, then just add a few drops of soy sauce to spice it up. The dish is successful because all the flavours you need are in the vegetables, accompanying the natural flavour of the fish.

Whole sautéed herrings and mustard sauce is a real British Classic, but it was always rather hard to eat the fish itself, with all those bones. I've adapted the recipe to make the fish easier to handle, and hopefully better to eat. The fish have been filleted and as many bones as possible removed, which immediately makes life a lot easier. The braised lentils aren't particularly traditional, but they eat very well with mustard, and add a whole new texture to the dish.

The fresh tuna dish is very summery in feel, with a warm onion and potato salad. The fish would taste wonderful if cooked over barbecue coals in the garden, but of course can be grilled or pan-fried in the kitchen.

There are many books with detailed instructions on how to scale, fillet and skin fish. But do remember that you can ask your fishmonger to prepare fish for you. He is an expert, will do it more quickly, and if he wants a return visit, he'll do it willingly. This will make it all much easier for you. Ask for a few extra bones to take home and make into a stock.

Cod with a Parsley Crust

The cod for this recipe is best cut from the middle of large fillets, giving good, thick, rectangular pieces of fish. The best way to serve the fish is sitting on a bed of mashed potatoes with a lemon butter sauce around (see p. 71). Finishing the dish this way creates three complementary textures with the crust, the fish and the potatoes.

SERVES 4

75 g (3 oz) unsalted butter
2 shallots, finely chopped
4 tablespoons chopped fresh parsley
½ large white sliced loaf, crusts removed
    and crumbed
Salt and freshly ground white pepper
4 cod fillet pieces, each about 175–225 g
    (6–8 oz)

To serve

1 quantity Mashed Potatoes (see p. 142)
1 quantity Lemon Butter Sauce (see
    p. 243)

Pre-heat the grill to medium, pre-heat the oven to 180–200°C/350–400°F/gas 4–6, and butter and season a flameproof dish.

Melt the butter with the chopped shallots, which should just soften them, then remove from the heat. Add the chopped parsley to the breadcrumbs and season with salt and pepper. Gradually mix this with the shallot butter to form a light paste. Place the fish on the prepared dish and cover each cod fillet with the parsley crust. Cook the cod under the grill, not too near the heat. It will take about 8–10 minutes. As the crust slowly colours, the fish will be cooking. When the fish under the crust turns opaque and milky and the crust is golden brown, it is ready. Finish in the pre-heated oven for a few minutes to make sure the fish is completely cooked.

Divide the mashed potatoes between four hot plates, sit the fish on top and spoon the warm sauce around.

Cod with Cabbage, Bacon and Peas

This dish holds all the simplest ingredients, yet is packed with textures and tastes. We all keep cabbage, bacon and peas, so all you have to do now is buy the cod.

SERVES 4

4 smoked back bacon rashers, rinded and cut into strips
2 onions, finely shredded
100 g (4 oz) unsalted butter
1 tablespoon olive oil
600 ml (1 pint) Chicken Stock (see p. 228)
½ green cabbage, finely shredded

100 g (4 oz) cooked fresh or frozen peas
Salt and freshly ground white pepper
1 tablespoon plain flour
4 cod fillet pieces, each about 175–225 g (6–8 oz), skinned
A little vegetable oil

To serve

1 quantity Mashed Potatoes (see p. 142)

Cook the bacon and onions in 25 g (1 oz) of the butter and the olive oil until soft. Add the chicken stock and bring to the boil. Allow to simmer for a few minutes then re-boil and add the cabbage. This will only need to cook for a few minutes until it is tender but with a little bite to it; it must be kept boiling to prevent the cabbage from stewing. Now add the peas and 50 g (2 oz) of the remaining butter in pieces. Check for seasoning.

Lightly flour the skinned side of the cod and brush with the remaining soft butter. Brush a frying-pan with a little oil. Pan-fry the cod, skinned side down, for about 5–6 minutes. The underside, or skinned side, is the presentation side.

Divide the hot mashed potato between four hot plates. Sit the fish on top of the potato and spoon the broth and vegetables around.

Grilled Sea Bass with Fettucine and Ratatouille Sauce

This is a very colourful dish which features many styles – English, Italian and French – many textures and, of course, many flavours. If you do not have the time to make your own pasta, there are many good-quality fresh and dried pastas available in the shops.

SERVES 4

450 g (1 lb) Pasta Dough (see p. 249)	4 sea bass fillets, each about
50 g (2 oz) unsalted butter	175–225 g (6–8 oz)
Salt and freshly ground black pepper	25 ml (1 fl oz) olive oil

For the Ratatouille Sauce

1 red pepper, seeded	25 g (1 oz) unsalted butter
1 green pepper, seeded	25 ml (1 fl oz) olive oil
2 shallots	300 ml (10 fl oz) Red Pepper Coulis
½ aubergine	(see p. 240)
1 courgette	

To make the fettucine, roll the dough through a pasta machine several times until it becomes about 1 mm (1/16 in) thick, then pass through the noodle cutter and leave to rest. If you do not have a pasta machine, it can be divided, rolled several times until very thin then cut by hand into ribbons; a pizza wheel is the easiest way to cut the pasta.

Pre-heat the grill to medium and butter and season a flameproof baking tray.

To make the ratatouille, cut the vegetables into 5 mm (¼ in) dice. Melt the butter with the olive oil in a large pan. Add the diced vegetables and cook for about 3–4 minutes until just softened. In another pan, warm the red pepper coulis then add the vegetables. Season with salt and pepper.

Lay the sea bass fillets on the prepared tray skin side up and cook under the medium grill for about 8 minutes.

While the fish is cooking, boil a large pan of water with the olive oil and a pinch of salt. When boiling, drop in the pasta and move it around with a fork. If it is fresh, it will only take a few minutes to cook. For dried pasta, just follow the instructions on the packet. Drain through a colander, season with salt and pepper and toss with the remaining butter to loosen.

Warm the ratatouille sauce and spoon it on to hot plates. Sit the fettucine in the middle and lay the grilled sea bass on the top.

Steamed Fillet of Turbot on Green Vegetables with Ginger and Lime

Once you have all the ingredients together for this, it's so quick and easy to cook. This is my own version of a Chinese stir-fry for fish. If you find turbot too expensive or difficult to buy, you can substitute cod, or any of your favourite fish.

SERVES 4

4 turbot fillets, each about 175 g (6 oz)
Salt and freshly ground white pepper
150 ml (5 fl oz) dry white wine
50 g (2 oz) unsalted butter or goose fat
450 g (1 lb) oyster or button mushrooms, sliced
450 g (1 lb) leeks, sliced

450 g (1 lb) fresh spinach, stalks removed
½ teaspoon grated fresh root ginger
½ bunch of fresh flatleaf parsley, picked
8 asparagus spears, blanched and cut into 5 cm (2 in) lengths
Juice of 1 lime

Pre-heat the oven to 220°C/425°F/gas 7 and grease and season a shallow baking tray. Place the turbot fillets in the tray, add the white wine and cover with buttered greaseproof paper. Place the tray into the pre-heated oven and the fish will begin to steam. They will take only 5–6 minutes to cook and will be just firm to the touch.

Meanwhile, heat a wok or frying-pan and add the butter or goose fat. Add the sliced mushrooms, leeks, spinach and ginger and stir-fry for about 2–3 minutes until almost cooked. Add the parsley and asparagus, season with salt and pepper and add the lime juice.

To serve, divide the vegetables between four hot plates. Sit the turbot on top of the vegetables and spoon a little of the fish cooking liquor over the top.

*Grilled Tuna
on Potato and
Onion Salad*

Grilled Tuna
on Potato and Onion Salad

Fresh tuna is a beautiful, meaty fish, but if you would prefer not to use it or just can't find anywhere to buy it, this dish can work very well with turbot, brill, bass and many other fish. The tuna medallions have a very similar texture to fillet of beef, and are cooked in a similar fashion. Tuna fillet eats best when cooked medium rare to medium.

SERVES 4

8 large onions, sliced
2 tablespoons water
350 g (12 oz) new potatoes, boiled
175–200 ml (6–7 fl oz) Basic Vinaigrette (see p. 245)

A few fresh basil and tarragon leaves, chopped
4 medallions of tuna fillet, each about 175 g (6 oz)
1 curly endive, separated, or a handful of lettuce leaves per person

Place the onions in a pan and allow to cook very slowly until the natural sugar from the onions starts to caramelize and then brown, stirring occasionally. This will take at least 1 hour of slow cooking.

Pre-heat the barbecue or grill to hot. Slice the warm new potatoes and sprinkle liberally with some of the vinaigrette. Mix with the onions and chopped herbs. This mixture should be kept just slightly warm.

The tuna would now best be cooked on an open barbecue to give a good grilled taste, but it can also be cooked under a pre-heated grill (or pan-fried in some butter and olive oil). It will take about 3–4 minutes per side, depending on the thickness of the fillet.

Spoon the potato and onion salad on to the centre of the plates. Dress the salad leaves with the remaining vinaigrette. Sit some leaves on top of the potatoes and finish with the tuna. Spoon some of the dressing over and serve.

Grilled Herrings with Braised Lentils and Mustard Seed Sauce

Grilled herrings whole on the bone with a separate hot English mustard sauce was one of the very first dishes I was taught as a young chef. They were very nice to eat, but hard work. So, to simplify everything for the diner, I decided to take them off the bone and try them just with the sauce. I then needed something to eat with them, and mashed potatoes worked very well, but I find lentils even tastier.

SERVES 4

8 large herring fillets

For the Braised Lentils

50 g (2 oz) unsalted butter
25 g (1 oz) carrot, finely diced
25 g (1 oz) celery, finely diced
25 g (1 oz) onion, finely diced
25 g (1 oz) leek, finely diced
1 small garlic clove, crushed

100 g (4 oz) green lentils (*lentilles de Puys*)
450 ml (15 fl oz) Chicken Stock (see p. 228) or Vegetable Stock (see p. 229)
Salt and freshly ground black pepper

For the Mustard Seed Sauce

2 shallots, finely chopped
1 celery stick, chopped
½ leek, chopped
1 bay leaf
50 g (2 oz) unsalted butter

300 ml (10 fl oz) dry white wine
600 ml (1 pint) Fish Stock (see p. 227)
300 ml (10 fl oz) double cream
About 2 teaspoons Meaux grain mustard

Pre-heat the oven to 200°C/400°F/gas 6 and butter and season a small flameproof baking tray.

To cook the lentils, melt the butter in a small ovenproof braising pan. Add the diced vegetables and garlic and cook for a few minutes. Add the lentils, stirring well. Cover with the stock and bring to the simmer. Cover with a lid and braise in the pre-heated oven for about 30–35 minutes until the lentils are tender and all the stock has been absorbed. Make sure they are tender before taking them from the oven. Season with salt and pepper.

To make the sauce, sweat the vegetables and bay leaf in the butter for a few minutes. Add the white wine and boil to reduce until almost dry. Add the fish stock and continue to boil until reduced by three-quarters. Pour on the cream and cook slowly until the sauce is thick enough to coat the back of a spoon. Strain through a fine sieve. Stir in the mustard a teaspoon at a time until the right taste is achieved, mustardy but not overpowering.

To cook the herring fillets, place them on to a greased baking tray and brush with butter. Cook under the hot grill for about 5–6 minutes. As soon as the fillets have coloured they will be ready to serve.

To serve, spoon the lentils on to the centre of four hot plates, pour the mustard sauce around and sit the fillets on top of the lentils. The dish is now complete!

Fillet of Red Mullet on Tapenade Toasts

Red mullet is perfect for this dish, which looks and certainly tastes very good and very Mediterranean. I particularly like to use an onion bread for the toasts.

SERVES 4

4 red mullet fillets, each about 175 g
   (6 oz), scaled and all bones removed
25 g (1 oz) unsalted butter, melted
Salt and freshly ground black pepper
4 slices onion or crusty bread
4 tablespoons Tapenade (see opposite)
½ curly endive, separated into leaves
150 ml (5 fl oz) Vierge Dressing (see
   p. 249)
2 tomatoes, skinned, seeded and diced
6 fresh basil leaves, chopped

Pre-heat the grill to hot and butter a flameproof tray. Lay the mullet fillets on the buttered tray, skin side up, brush with the butter and season with salt and pepper. Place the fish under the hot grill and allow the red skin to crisp. This will only take 3–4 minutes.

Toast the slices of bread and spread the tapenade on to each slice. Place the toasts on hot plates. Toss the curly endive in a little of the vierge dressing and sit on top of the toasts. Place the fillets on top of the lettuce. Mix the diced tomatoes and basil with the remaining vierge dressing and spoon over and around the fish.

Tapenade

Tapenade comes from the word tapeno with means 'caper' in Provençal. This paste is absolutely delicious and can be used for so many things. I like to spread it on toast to serve with the red mullet dish, left, but it is also great just to have on toast as a snack with drinks.

MAKES about 350 g (12 oz)

225 g (8 oz) black olives, stoned
1 small garlic clove, crushed
50 g (2 oz) tinned anchovy fillets, drained
25 g (1 oz) capers, drained
2 tablespoons olive oil
1 teaspoon lemon juice
Freshly ground black pepper

Place the olives, garlic, anchovies and capers into a food processor and blitz to a purée. While the motor is still running, slowly add the olive oil until the mix is pliable. You may need a little more olive oil. Add the lemon juice and season to taste with pepper. The tapenade is now ready to use or will keep for about a week in the fridge.

Fingers of Skate
with Potatoes, Fennel and
Braised Artichokes

This dish really doesn't have to be difficult. The potatoes and fennel are quick and easy to prepare, and if the artichokes sound like too much hard work (but it's worth a try), there are good-quality tinned artichoke bottoms available. Mixed bags of salad leaves are also available in supermarkets.

SERVES 4

225 g (8 oz) new potatoes, boiled
1 onion, finely chopped
100 ml (3½ fl oz) Basic Vinaigrette
   (see p. 245)
2 fennel bulbs, trimmed
Salt and freshly ground white
   pepper
Juice of ½ lemon

1 quantity Braised Artichoke Bottoms
   (see opposite)
50 g (2 oz) unsalted butter
700 g (1½ lb) skate wing fillets
Plain flour for coating
1 tablespoon olive oil
A handful of green salad leaves (rocket,
   curly endive, lamb's lettuce etc.)

For the Dressing

1 egg
25 g (1 oz) capers, drained
6 tinned anchovy fillets, drained
1 garlic clove
1 × 2.5 cm (1 in) piece fresh ginger root,
   peeled
1 bunch of fresh basil leaves

Juice of 1 lemon
½ teaspoon chopped fresh thyme
A pinch of sugar
50 ml (2 fl oz) warm water
225 ml (7½ fl oz) olive oil
225 ml (7½ fl oz) ground-nut oil
Salt and freshly ground black pepper

To make the dressing, place all the ingredients except the oils into a food processor and blitz to a paste. With the motor running, slowly add the oil, as you would for mayonnaise. Push the dressing through a fine sieve then season to taste with salt and pepper.

Slice the new potatoes while still warm and mix with the chopped onion. Add about 2 tablespoons of the vinaigrette to moisten.

To cook the fennel, plunge it into boiling, salted water with the lemon juice and simmer for about 20 minutes until tender. Allow to cool in the liquor. When cool, halve the fennel and slice into long strips.

Warm the potatoes, fennel and artichokes together in half the butter.

Cut the skate into fingers, allowing five pieces per portion. Lightly flour the skate and fry in the remaining butter and the olive oil for a few minutes on each side.

Mix the dressing with the potatoes, fennel and artichokes and spoon on to the centre of the plates. Sit the skate fingers on top and finish with some salad leaves tossed in the remaining vinaigrette. Any left-over dressing can be kept in the fridge and used for simple mixed salads.

Braised Artichoke Bottoms

There are so many things you can do with artichoke bottoms, from adding them to a mixed salad to stuffing and braising. This recipe will help you cook them, the rest is up to you.

SERVES 4

2 large globe artichokes	1 tablespoon olive oil
Juice of ½ lemon	1 bay leaf
1 shallot, chopped	1 sprig of fresh thyme
1 carrot, chopped	6 black peppercorns
1 celery stick, chopped	6 coriander seeds
25 g (1 oz) unsalted butter	4 tomatoes, chopped

Firstly remove the stalks from the artichokes and then cut around the base, removing the leaves. Now cut across about 4 cm (1½ in) from the base and cut off any excess stalk or green left on. The centre of the bottom will still be intact. Rub with lemon juice.

Sweat the chopped shallot, carrot and celery in the butter and olive oil for a few minutes, then add the bay leaf, thyme, peppercorns, coriander seeds and chopped tomatoes. Pour in just enough water to cover. Bring to a simmer and cook for 10 minutes. Add the artichoke bottoms and about 1 teaspoon of lemon juice and simmer for 20–30 minutes until tender. When cooked and cooled, remove and discard the bristly centres. Cut each bottom in half, and each half into four or five slices. They are now ready to use.

Salmon Fish Cakes (see p. 88) served with Lemon Butter Sauce (see p. 243)

66 *These are fish cakes with a difference.* **99**

Salmon Fish Cakes

These are fish cakes with a difference. They are simple to make, but good to look at and great to eat (see previous page). They go very well with a green salad.

SERVES 4–6

2 shallots, finely chopped
Salt and freshly ground white pepper
450 g (1 lb) salmon, filleted and skinned
1 tablespoon unsalted butter
150 ml (5 fl oz) dry white wine
1 tablespoon chopped fresh parsley
350 g (12 oz) Mashed Potatoes without
   cream or butter (see p. 142)

2 tablespoons plain flour
2 eggs, beaten
100 g (4 oz) fresh breadcrumbs for
   coating
Vegetable oil for deep-frying
1 quantity Lemon Butter Sauce
   (see p. 243)

Pre-heat the oven to 200°C/400°F/gas 6 and butter and season a baking tray.

Sprinkle the finely chopped shallots on to the prepared baking tray, sit the salmon on top and season again with salt and pepper. Add the white wine, cover with foil and cook in the pre-heated oven for about 8–10 minutes until the fish is just cooked. The salmon should be just firm on the outside and still pink in the middle.

Sit the salmon in a colander over a pan to collect all the cooking juices. When all the juices have been collected, boil to reduce them to a syrupy consistency.

Break up the salmon with a wooden spoon, then add the syrupy reduction and the chopped parsley. Fold in 225 g (8 oz) of the potato, and then add it a spoonful at a time until you have a binding texture. Check for seasoning then roll into 12 to 18 balls about 4 cm (1½ in) in diameter. Three cakes per portion will be enough. Lightly pass through the flour, beaten eggs and then the breadcrumbs; repeat the process of egg and breadcrumbs once more.

The fish cakes are now ready for deep-frying which cooks them well and gives a good all-round colour. Heat the vegetable oil to 180°C/350°F then fry the fish cakes for about 4–5 minutes. Drain well on kitchen paper.

To serve, just pour the warm lemon butter sauce into individual serving dishes or bowls and sit three fish cakes in the middle of each one.

Poultry and Meat

It is in this section of the main course recipes that we can start to imagine that murmuring and bubbling *daube* mentioned at the beginning of the book. And it is here that you will find most of the basic techniques of Great Old British cookery that have become so much a personal and professional passion.

Some of the recipes are what you might expect – Braised Oxtail, Beef Stew and Dumplings, Boiled Bacon, Irish Stew and Lancashire Hot-pot. But a couple are a little different, using cuts of meat that are not eaten so much now – although in the good old days they were very popular. Faggots are a regional dish using kidney, liver and ox heart wrapped in caul fat (just like the classic French *crépinettes*); they're delicious with my Onion Gravy. Pigs' cheeks should not be too difficult to find. They are pure meat, and when braised are so succulent and tasty – I think they are a lot more flavoursome than pork chops, loins or even fillets. If you can't get them, just substitute chunks of pork; it's not quite the same, but the recipe still works. When they have been slowly braised, they're so soft and tender. You might find some difficulty in obtaining lambs' tongues but this is where having a good, friendly and understanding butcher comes in handy.

Most dishes here are on the British theme, apart from one or two. The Confit of Duck and all its variations are French, as is the Jambonette de Volaille. The Chicken with Paprika, Lemon and Soy Sauce is eastern in flavour, the Chicken Breast with Noodles and the Fillets of Lamb on Aubergine more Italian.

There's still plenty of room for all those dishes from the various culinary roads that criss-cross Britain: faggots from the west and Wales; steak and kidney pudding from the north, along with sausages and our boiled bacon. Although the boiled bacon is my own recipe, I've found a very similar Cumbrian version which uses orange lentils and split peas instead of green lentils and pearl barley.

One of my own favourite British specialities is the good old Cornish pasty, but when I published my own version under that name in a newspaper article, I was inundated with letters saying mine was nothing like the real thing. So I now call my version a Home-made Lamb Pasty! Apparently, or so I'm told, the way to test a real Cornish pasty is to drop it 100 feet down a mine; if the pastry doesn't break, then it's genuine!

Chicken with Wild Mushrooms, Grapes and Tarragon

This dish can be a fricassee, as here, or the chicken can simply be roasted and the sauce served separately. Oyster or pleurote mushrooms have become fairly common, but if you have any problem finding them, just substitute with button mushrooms.

SERVES 4

1 chicken, 1.5–1.75 kg (3–4 lb)	25 g (1 oz) unsalted butter
350 g (12 oz) oyster or button mushrooms	1 tablespoon olive oil
	175 g (6 oz) seedless grapes, peeled
1 bunch of fresh tarragon	Salt and freshly ground white pepper

For the Sauce

4 shallots, chopped	50 g (2 oz) unsalted butter
1 carrot, chopped	300 ml (10 fl oz) dry white wine
2 celery sticks, chopped	1.2 litres (2 pints) Chicken Stock (see
1 bay leaf	p. 228)
1 sprig of fresh thyme	450 ml (15 fl oz) double cream

For a fricassee, the chicken must be cut into four portions, removing the breasts and legs from the carcass. Split the drumsticks from the thighs, but leave the breasts whole. The carcass should be chopped and used in making the sauce.

Pre-heat the oven to 200°C/400°F/gas 6.

Pick over the oyster mushrooms, removing and reserving the stalks, and slice the mushroom caps. Remove the stalks from the tarragon and reserve them for the sauce.

To make the sauce, sweat the tarragon stalks, chopped shallots, carrot, celery, bay leaf and thyme in half the butter. Add the chopped chicken carcass and the mushroom trimmings and cook for a few minutes. Pour on the white wine and boil to reduce until almost dry. Add the chicken stock and boil to reduce by three-quarters. Add the cream and simmer for 20 minutes. Strain the sauce through a sieve.

Fry the chicken pieces in the butter and olive oil until coloured then transfer to the pre-heated oven and cook for 20 minutes, checking the breasts after 10 minutes; they may be ready and can be removed. When the chicken is cooked, leave it to rest for 15 minutes. Add the sliced mushroom caps, tarragon leaves and grapes to the sauce and warm them through until the mushrooms are tender. Season with salt and pepper.

Cut the chicken breasts in half and divide the chicken, giving a piece of breast and leg for each portion. Spoon over the sauce and serve.

Chicken with Paprika, Lemon and Soy Sauce

This dish eats very well with my Mashed Potatoes (see p. 142), which can be spiced up with a little olive oil, chopped onion, garlic, even chopped parsley for that extra taste and colour.

SERVES 4

1 chicken, about 1.5–1.75 kg (3½–4 lb)	2 heaped tablespoons paprika
1 garlic clove, halved	2 tablespoons plain flour
150 ml (5 fl oz) olive oil	Juice of 3 lemons
Salt and freshly ground white pepper	50 ml (2 fl oz) soy sauce
1 sprig of fresh thyme, chopped	50 g (2 oz) unsalted butter

Pre-heat the oven to 220°C/425°F/gas 7.

Cut the chicken into eight pieces: split the legs in half; remove the breasts from the carcass and cut each into two pieces. Rub the chicken pieces with the garlic and some of the olive oil. Season with salt and pepper and sprinkle with chopped thyme. Mix the paprika and flour together and cover the chicken pieces liberally with the mixture. Mix together the lemon juice and soy sauce and cover the chicken with half of this mixture.

Pre-heat a large flameproof baking pan and add some of the olive oil and half the butter. Add the chicken and fry over a high heat to crisp the skin until it is almost burnt black. Turn the chicken pieces in the pan and add the remaining lemon juice and soy sauce and a little more of the paprika mix. Place in the pre-heated oven for about 20 minutes, by which time the chicken will have a very crispy skin.

Remove the chicken from the pan and drain the liquor through a sieve into another pan. Warm this liquor and add the remaining butter. The sauce will now almost have a sweet and sour taste from the lemon, soy sauce and paprika. Simply pour it over the chicken and serve. Or, if you are serving the dish with mashed potatoes, divide the potato between individual plates, sit the chicken on top and pour the juices over.

Grilled Chicken Breast with Noodles in Creamy Mushroom Sauce

This is a variation on a great old Italian classic: noodles, mushrooms and a cream sauce (see p. 119 and pp. 230–1). It's a great way of turning a simple chicken breast into a wonderful dish, and is best served with a mixed or green salad. The marinated chicken breasts can be cooked on an open barbecue and served with a salad, and the cream sauce can be used with other dishes, even just with noodles on their own. If you don't have time to make your own fettucine, you can use shop-bought fresh or dried.

SERVES 4

4 chicken breasts
Salt and freshly ground white pepper
450 g (1 lb) Fettucine (see p. 76)
A little olive oil
1 teaspoon chopped fresh parsley

For the Marinade

300 ml (10 fl oz) olive oil
Juice of 2 lemons
1 garlic clove, crushed

½ teaspoon chopped fresh thyme
½ teaspoon chopped fresh basil
½ teaspoon chopped fresh tarragon

For the Cream Sauce

4 chicken wings (optional)
1 carrot, coarsely chopped
1 onion, coarsely chopped
2 celery sticks, coarsely chopped
1 small leek, coarsely chopped
50 g (2 oz) unsalted butter
1 small garlic clove

1 sprig of fresh thyme
1 bay leaf
A few fresh basil leaves
300 ml (10 fl oz) dry white wine
900 ml (1½ pints) Chicken Stock
    (see p. 228)
600 ml (1 pint) double cream

For the Garnish

2 large onions, sliced
6 smoked back bacon rashers, rinded
    and chopped
225 g (8 oz) button mushrooms, sliced
50 g (2 oz) unsalted butter

Mix together all the marinade ingredients, season with salt and pepper and pour over the chicken breasts. The breasts are best left in the marinade for 48 hours to allow them to take on the tastes.

Pre-heat the grill to medium.

To make the cream sauce, cook the chicken wings and chopped vegetables in the butter with the garlic and herbs until softened. Add the white wine and boil to reduce until almost dry. Add the chicken stock and boil to reduce by two-thirds. Add the cream, slowly bring to the simmer then simmer the sauce gently for about 30 minutes. Push the sauce through a sieve, check for seasoning and keep to one side in a large pan.

Remove the chicken breasts from the marinade and grill them until cooked through and tender, or pan-fry them in a little butter and olive oil.

The pasta can be made as for the sea bass recipe (see p. 76), or finer spaghetti noodles can be made or bought for this. It just needs to be boiled in salted water with a little oil until tender.

For the garnish, cook the sliced onions, bacon and mushrooms in the butter until they are soft.

To serve, place the pasta and garnish into the sauce, bring to the simmer and allow it to warm through for 2 minutes. Divide the pasta and garnish between four large bowls and spoon some of the sauce over each one. The grilled or pan-fried chicken can now be carved into two pieces, cutting at an angle through the middle. Slightly divide the chicken and sit it on top of the noodles. Pour 8–10 tablespoons of the marinade through a sieve into a bowl and add the chopped parsley. Spoon a little over each chicken breast just before serving.

66*The preparation is as important as the cooking.* 99

Dicing the bacon for Jambonette de Volaille (see p. 96).

Jambonette de Volaille

This is a classic French dish and really is just a stuffed chicken leg. When totally finished, the shape resembles a small ham, which is where the name jambonette *comes from (see pp. 70–1). This recipe may look time-consuming, but it is very straightforward and worth every effort. The jambonette eats well with Braised Butter Beans (see p. 99) Ratatouille (see p. 76), or Tomato and Onion Flavoured Gravy (see p. 239).*

Serves 4

4 chicken legs
225 g (8 oz) pig's caul, soaked in cold
　　water for 24 hours (optional)
2 tablespoons olive oil

For the Stuffing

225 g (8 oz) button mushrooms, minced
　　or finely chopped
2 small chicken breasts, skinned
50 g (2 oz) fresh spinach, stalks removed,
　　blanched and drained
1 large onion, finely chopped
2 smoked bacon rashers, rinded and
　　finely diced

1 garlic clove, crushed
A few fresh basil leaves, chopped
100 g (4 oz) oyster mushrooms
　　(optional), sliced
25 g (1 oz) unsalted butter
Salt and freshly ground white
　　pepper
1 egg

To serve

Braised Butter Beans (see p. 99) or
　　Ratatouille (see p. 76)
Tomato and Onion Flavoured Gravy
　　(see p. 239)

Firstly, the chicken legs must be boned. Lay the leg, skin side down, and cut along the thigh bone only. Scrape down the bone towards the joint and the thigh meat will start to fall from the bone. Continue to scrape until the bone is free of any meat. Keep the point of the knife close to the knuckle joint and cut round carefully. The joint will now be clean. Continue the same process and scrape down to the next joint. At this point, the bone can be broken or cut and the leg will be boned. Repeat the same process for all the legs, just leaving the knuckle on the end of each one.

To make the stuffing, heat the minced mushrooms on their own in a pan until they become totally dry. Allow to cool. Mince or finely chop the chicken breasts with the blanched spinach then mix into the mushrooms and chill in the fridge. Heat the onion, bacon, garlic, basil and oyster mushrooms, if using, in the butter for a few minutes until softened, then allow to cool. Add to the chicken and mushroom mixture, season with salt and pepper and mix in the egg.

Fill the boned legs with the stuffing, filling them enough to re-shape into a chicken leg, and folding the skin and meat under to seal the leg. They can now be wrapped in pig's caul, if using, or simply use wooden cocktail sticks to hold the legs together. Leave the legs to rest for at least 1 hour in the fridge to set, then they will be ready to roast.

Pre-heat the oven to 200°C/400°F/gas 6.

Fry the legs on the curved side in the olive oil in a flameproof baking pan until golden brown then turn in the pan and cook in the pre-heated oven for 20–25 minutes.

Serve the hot butter beans or ratatouille on to hot plates. Cut the jambonette into 4–5 slices and arrange on the beans or vegetables and serve with the tomato and onion sauce poured around.

Confit of Duck

Confit comes from the French word meaning 'to preserve'. It is a classic regional dish from Gascony in south-west France. The technique can be applied to various different meats, but duck, goose and pork are the most common. So many tastes and textures can be achieved in the dish, but it will, of course, depend on how long you marinate the meat, how slowly you cook it, how you store it and what actually goes into the marinade. I'm going to give you my version, with various ways of serving it. I cook it in goose fat, which is quite expensive to buy, but the dish will work very well with rendered pork fat or lard. It really is worth making the effort for a good confit. The recipes that follow are just a few ideas of what to eat with confit. If you don't fancy any of these, confit is wonderful with a good salad.

SERVES 4

4 duck legs
2 teaspoons rock salt
1–1.5 kg (2–3 lb) goose or pork fat to
    cover
4 tablespoons clear honey

For the Marinade

A few sprigs of fresh thyme
1 bay leaf
6 fresh basil leaves
12 black peppercorns
1 garlic clove, sliced
2 shallots or 1 onion,
    chopped

2.5 cm (1 in) fresh root ginger, peeled
    and grated
2 teaspoons Worcestershire sauce
2 teaspoons soy sauce
2 teaspoons balsamic vinegar
1 tablespoon white wine vinegar
1 tablespoon extra virgin olive oil

Mix together all the ingredients for the marinade. Rub each duck leg with the rock salt. Place the legs in the marinade, cover and leave for at least 3–4 days in the fridge. The longer the legs marinate, the stronger the flavour will become.

Pre-heat the oven to 160–180°C/325–350°F/gas 3–4.

To cook the duck legs, melt the fat in a deep flameproof baking dish or tray. Add the duck legs to the fat and cook in the pre-heated oven for about 2 hours. When cooked slowly the legs take on more flavour. Check them during cooking: if you try to separate the leg from the thigh and it starts to give easily, then they are ready. Leave to cool in the fat.

The legs can be eaten immediately after cooking. Or at this stage, they can be transferred to a suitable container, covered with the cooking fat and chilled. They will keep for weeks, even months, and the flavour will be developing all the time. When you are ready to serve them, simply remove them from the fat and cook in the low oven for about 20 minutes. I always like to finish my confit with a tablespoon of honey on each leg and then crisp it under the grill.

Braised Butter Beans

Braised butter beans go well with many other dishes as well as confit (see pp. 70–1).

SERVES 4

1 onion, chopped
2 smoked bacon rashers, rinded and cut into strips
1 tablespoon olive oil
1 tablespoon unsalted butter
1 garlic clove, crushed
8 fresh basil leaves, chopped

1 bay leaf
100 g (4 oz) dried butter beans
600–900 ml (1–1½ pints) Chicken Stock (see p. 228)
2 tomatoes, skinned, seeded and diced
Salt and freshly ground black pepper

To serve

A few curly endive leaves
1 quantity Confit of Duck (see left)
2–3 tablespoons Basic Vinaigrette (see p. 245)
1 quantity Red Wine Sauce (see p. 236)

Pre-heat the oven to 180°C/350°F/gas 4.

Sweat the chopped onion and bacon in a flameproof dish in the olive oil and butter for a few minutes, then add the garlic, basil, bay leaf and butter beans. Cover with 600 ml (1 pint) of chicken stock and bring to the simmer. Cover and cook in the pre-heated oven for 1–1½ hours until the beans are tender; they may need a little more stock added during the cooking process.

When the beans are tender they will have created a thick sauce. Add the tomatoes, salt and pepper and spoon on to hot plates. Mix the curly endive with the vinaigrette and sit some on top of the beans. Finish with the hot, glazed duck confit and pour some red wine sauce around.

Confit of Duck
with Cabbage, Onions and
Beansprouts

The flavours in the dish give an oriental taste similar to the classic Peking duck.

SERVES 4

½ green cabbage, shredded
225 g (8 oz) beansprouts
2 onions, sliced
25 g (1 oz) goose fat or unsalted butter
2 tablespoons olive oil
Salt and freshly ground black pepper
A pinch of five-spice powder
300 ml (10 fl oz) Veal *Jus* (see p. 232) or
　　bought alternative (see p. 225)
1 quantity Confit of Duck (see p. 98)
1–3 tablespoons Plum Purée Sauce
　　(see p. 242)

Blanch the cabbage and beansprouts separately in boiling salted water then refresh under cold water and drain well. Fry the onions in the goose fat or butter and olive oil until softened and brown. Add the cabbage and beansprouts and season with salt, pepper and five-spice powder. Continue to cook for 3–4 minutes until slightly softened.

Bring the veal *jus* to the simmer and gradually add the plum purée sauce until a rich, spicy plum flavour is achieved. One tablespoon may well be enough, the quantity all depends on your taste buds.

Spoon the cabbage mixture on to the hot plates, sit the hot, glazed confit on top and pour the sauce around.

Confit of Duck with Red Cabbage and Apples

SERVES 4

4 apples, peeled and cored
½ red cabbage, shredded
2 onions, sliced
65 g (2½ oz) unsalted butter
150 ml (5 fl oz) red wine vinegar
25 g (1 oz) demerara sugar
150 ml (5 fl oz) red wine
Salt and freshly ground black pepper

To serve

1 quantity Confit of Duck (see p. 98)
1 quantity Red Wine Sauce (see p. 236)

Chop two of the apples. Sweat the red cabbage and onions in 50 g (2 oz) of the butter for a few minutes until softened. Add the chopped apples and cook for a further few minutes. Add the wine vinegar and cook until it evaporates. Add the sugar and red wine and season with salt and pepper. Cover with a lid and continue to cook for about 30 minutes until the cabbage is tender.

Slice the remaining apples in to 12 rings. Melt the remaining butter and fry the apple rings in a hot pan, browning on both sides.

Spoon the cabbage on to hot plates and sit three apple rings on top. Arrange the hot, glazed duck confit on the apples and pour the red wine sauce around.

Calves' Liver with Onion Gravy and Mashed Potatoes

This has to be the most popular main course on my menu. It's simple, it's tasty, but of course calves' liver isn't the easiest offal to find. I also enjoy lambs' liver, so this recipe can be used with the liver of your choice. The liver also eats very well with the bacon just plain, without the sauce or potatoes. You can then serve your own choice of vegetables to go with it.

SERVES 4

700 g (1½ lb) calves' liver
700 g (1½ lb) Mashed Potatoes (see p. 142)
600 ml (1 pint) Onion Gravy (see p. 233)
4 smoked middle bacon rashers, rinded
50 g (2 oz) unsalted butter

The liver can be bought already sliced, but if you wish to cut your own, make sure the film of soft sinew covering the meat is removed first. Cut the liver into about eight thin slices.

Pre-heat the grill to hot.

Prepare the mashed potatoes and onion gravy and keep them hot on the stove. Grill the bacon until crispy.

The ideal way to cook the liver is on an open grill for the maximum taste. If you don't have a grill, pan-fried liver will be equally good. Pre-heat a frying-pan very hot. Add the butter and the liver. If the liver has been sliced 6 mm (¼ in) thick, it will only take 1½ minutes on both sides. It will now be a good colour and still slightly pink inside, making it moist to eat.

To serve the dish, spoon the potatoes towards the top of hot plates and cover the rest of the plate with onion gravy. Lay the liver on the potatoes and gravy, allowing two slices per portion. To finish, just sit the bacon rashers on top.

OPPOSITE
*Calves' Liver with Onion Gravy
and Mashed Potatoes.*

Faggots in Onion Gravy

I usually use the trimmings from cuts of beef for this when I make them (see pp. 106–7). Pig's caul (the lining of a pig's stomach) is the classic wrapping for faggots, and your butcher should be able to get some for you. (It needs to be soaked in cold water for 24 hours before use.) Alternatively, you can fry the faggots without the caul, as for meatballs, but the finish and flavour won't be quite the same. The best dishes to serve with faggots are Colcannon (see p. 142) or Mashed Potatoes (see p. 142).

SERVES 4

2 onions, finely chopped
1 garlic clove, crushed
½ teaspoon fresh thyme leaves
½ teaspoon chopped fresh sage
½ teaspoon chopped fresh parsley
50 g (2 oz) unsalted butter
300 ml (10 fl oz) Veal *Jus* (see p. 232) or
　bought alternative (see p. 225)

175 g (6 oz) lean beef rump or topside,
　well trimmed
175 g (6 oz) ox heart, trimmed
175 g (6 oz) ox kidney, trimmed
175 g (6 oz) lambs' liver, trimmed
Salt and freshly ground black pepper
1 egg
450 g (1 lb) pig's caul, soaked in cold
　water for 24 hours

To finish

1.2 litres (2 pints) thin Veal *Jus* or Stock
　(see p. 232)
25 g (1 oz) beef dripping
1 quantity Onion Gravy (see p. 233)

Cook the chopped onions, garlic and herbs in the butter until soft. Add the veal *jus* and boil to reduce by two-thirds. Leave to cool, then allow to set in the fridge.

Mince the meats through a medium cutter. Place all the minced meat in a mixer and beat slowly, adding salt and pepper to taste. The salt will also thicken the meat, giving a gelatinous texture. Add the egg and the reduced, cool onion mix. The faggot mixture is now ready, and is best left chilled for 2–3 hours to set more firmly.

To form the faggots, squeeze any excess water from the caul and cut it into 8 × 20 cm (8 in) squares. Spoon about 75 g (3 oz) of the faggot mixture into the centre of each square and wrap and turn the caul around the meat to form firm ball shapes.

When you are ready to cook the faggots, warm the veal *jus* or stock. Fry the faggots in the dripping until brown on all sides, then place them in the *jus* or stock and simmer very gently for 12–15 minutes until just starting to firm up. Remove the pan from the heat and leave to rest. The faggots can now be allowed to cool, left in the cooking liquor, and chilled. The liquor will set like a jelly and keep the faggots for up to a week in the fridge.

When you want to serve the faggots, remove them from the jelly and heat through for 15–20 minutes in the onion gravy on top of the stove. To serve, lift the faggots from the gravy and arrange on hot plates. Sit the onions on top and spoon over the gravy.

LEFT Stage 1:
Preparing the pig's caul.
RIGHT Stage 2:
Spooning in the filling.

LEFT Stage 3:
Rolling the faggot.

ABOVE
*Faggots simmering in
Onion Gravy
(see p. 104).*

Pigs' Cheeks Stew

Pigs' cheeks are certainly an unusual cut of meat, not very often used. You'll have to know your butcher and ask him to save some for you. What you want is just the meaty part of the cheek. This is a classic recipe for stewing them, but if cheeks are unavailable, replace with large chunks of lean pork. The cheeks are best served with Mashed Potatoes (see p. 142) and Glazed Carrots (see p. 161) or Spinach with Cream and Garlic (see p. 153).

SERVES 4

1.5 kg (3 lb) pigs' cheeks, trimmed of all sinews
Salt and freshly ground black pepper
50 g (2 oz) plain flour
25 g (1 oz) beef dripping or lard
450 g (1 lb) shallots or onions, sliced
225 g (8 oz) bacon rind, cut into strips
6 garlic cloves, halved

A few black peppercorns
1 bottle red wine
600 ml (1 pint) Veal *Jus* (see p. 232) or bought alternative (see p. 225)
1 bouquet garni (1 bay leaf, 1 sprig of fresh thyme, 2 sprigs of fresh sage wrapped and tied in a strip of leek) or bouquet garni sachet

For the Garnish

225 g (8 oz) button onions
100 g (4 oz) unsalted butter
225 g (8 oz) button mushrooms
175 g (6 oz) smoked bacon, rinded and cut into strips

Season the cheeks with salt and pepper and lightly dip in flour. Pre-heat the lard in a frying-pan and fry the cheeks until coloured on both sides. Remove from the pan and place in a large flameproof casserole. Add the sliced shallots or onions to the frying-pan and fry until tender. Transfer the shallots or onions to the casserole using a slotted spoon. Add the bacon rind to the frying-pan and fry for a few minutes then transfer to the casserole. Add the garlic and peppercorns to the frying-pan and pour on the red wine and *jus*. Bring to the simmer, then pour over the cheeks and add the bouquet garni. Cover and allow to cook gently for about 1½–2 hours until the cheeks are tender.

Meanwhile, prepare the garnish. Fry the button onions in the butter until softened and golden brown. Add the mushrooms and bacon strips and continue to fry for a few more minutes. Leave to drain of any excess fat in a sieve or colander.

When the cheeks are tender, remove them from the sauce and strain the sauce through a sieve into a pan. Boil the sauce until reduced to a thicker consistency, skimming once or twice, if necessary, to remove any impurities. Once re-boiled, mix with the cheeks again, add the drained garnishes and re-heat gently before serving.

Duck Variation

This recipe can also be used for duck legs. Allowing one leg per portion, simply remove the skin, separate the thigh from the drumstick and quickly fry in fat. Soak the legs in red wine and chill for a few days to enhance the taste, or cook straightaway as for the cheeks. The legs will take about 2 hours to cook in the liquor, and they eat particularly well with the Spinach with Cream and Garlic (see p. 153)

Braised Oxtail

This dish is more than just traditional British, in fact it has become my signature dish. I find it exciting to cook and even more exciting to eat. You can pick up the tails and eat them with your hands and just dip your bread in the sauce to collect all the tastes. The tails are also very good served with creamy Mashed Potatoes (see p. 142).

*Braised Oxtail
with Mashed Potatoes
(see p. 142).*

SERVES 4–6

4 oxtails, trimmed of fat
Salt and freshly ground black pepper
100 g (4 oz) beef dripping
225 g (8 oz) carrots, chopped
225 g (8 oz) onions, chopped
225 g (8 oz) celery sticks, chopped
225 g (8 oz) leeks, chopped

450 g (1 lb) tomatoes, chopped
1 sprig of fresh thyme
1 bay leaf
1 garlic clove, crushed
600 ml (1 pint) red wine
2.25 litres (4 pints) Veal Stock (see p. 232) or bought alternative (see p. 225)

For the Garnish

1 large carrot, finely diced
1 onion, finely diced
2 celery sticks, finely diced

1 leek, finely diced
6 tomatoes, skinned, seeded and diced
2 tablespoons chopped fresh parsley

For this recipe, the veal stock should not have been reduced to a sauce consistency, as this tends to become too strong when braising the tails. Oxtails can be used in place of veal bones when making the stock for extra beef flavour.

Pre-heat the oven to 200°C/400°F/gas 6.

Firstly, separate the trimmed tails between the joints and season with salt and pepper. In a large pan, fry the tails in the dripping until brown on all sides, then drain in a colander. Fry the chopped carrot, onion, celery and leek in the same pan, collecting all the residue from the tails. Add the chopped tomatoes, thyme, bay leaf and garlic and continue to cook for a few minutes. Place the tails in a large braising pan with the vegetables. Pour the red wine into the pan and boil to reduce until almost dry. Add some of the stock then pour on to the meat in the braising pan and cover with the remaining stock. Bring the tails to a simmer and braise in the pre-heated oven for 1½–2 hours until the meat is tender.

Lift the pieces of meat from the sauce and keep to one side. Push the sauce through a sieve into a pan, then boil to reduce it, skimming off all impurities, to a good sauce consistency.

While the sauce is reducing, quickly cook the diced garnish carrot, onion, celery and leek in a tablespoon of water until soft. When the sauce is ready, add the tails and vegetable garnish and simmer until the tails are warmed through. Add the diced tomato and spoon into hot bowls, allowing three or four oxtail pieces per portion. Sprinkle with chopped parsley and serve.

Braised Lambs' Tongues

Lambs' tongues are a cheap cut of meat which don't get used very often. They take a while to cook, but are simple and worth every minute. This recipe is similar to the Irish Stew (see p.129) in its basic ingredients, but there are many additions that can change the whole dish: Meaux mustard can be added at the end; mushrooms and bacon can be cooked with the vegetables; celeriac, swede and parsnip can all be used to lift the dish. This eats very well with the Mashed Potatoes (see p. 142) or just some crusty bread.

SERVES 4–6

12 lambs' tongues
1.75 litres (3 pints) Chicken Stock (see p. 228)
3 large onions
450 g (1 lb) carrots
8 celery sticks
675 g (1½ lb) potatoes, peeled
50 g (2 oz) unsalted butter

2 tablespoons olive oil
2 garlic cloves, crushed
1 bouquet garni (1 bay leaf, 1 sprig each of fresh thyme, rosemary and sage, wrapped and tied in a strip of leek) or bouquet garni sachet
Salt and freshly ground black pepper
1 tablespoon chopped fresh parsley

Cover the tongues with cold water in a large pan and bring to the boil. Drain, then refresh under cold water. Return the tongues to the same pan and cover with chicken stock. Bring to the simmer, cover and cook slowly for 2–2½ hours in the stock. Make sure they are covered with liquid all the time, adding more stock or water if necessary. Check after 2 hours. Remove one tongue from the stock and pinch or pierce with a knife; it will either give slightly or the knife will pierce easily if it is cooked. If not, continue to cook for a further 30 minutes then re-check. When cooked and still warm, remove them from the stock and take off the skins. These will peel off very easily. Strain and reserve the cooking liquor.

Cut the vegetables into 2.5 cm (1 in) pieces. Melt the butter and olive oil in a separate pan and cook the vegetables, garlic and bouquet garni for 5–10 minutes. Add the reserved cooking liquor, season with salt and pepper, bring to the simmer and cook for 15 minutes.

Cut the tongues into two or three pieces and add to the vegetables. Bring back to the simmer and continue to cook for a further 5–10 minutes. Remove the bouquet garni and taste for seasoning. Sprinkle with parsley and the stew is ready. The tongues will be tender and the vegetables will have taken on the flavours of the cooking liquor.

Boiled Bacon with Pearl Barley and Lentils

There are so many alternative ways of serving boiled bacon. It eats well with split peas, broad beans and even just parsley sauce, but this is one of my favourite ways of serving it. It could even be used as a winter soup. The bacon can also be served with Braised Split Peas (see p. 154), with just a little stock spooned over. Any left-over stock can be frozen for soup-making, some sauces, or even your next boiled bacon.

SERVES 4

1.8 kg (4 lb) unsmoked rolled bacon collar, rind removed	50 g (2 oz) pearl barley
5 carrots	1 large swede
4 onions	2 parsnips
2 celery sticks	100 g (4 oz) unsalted butter
1 leek	1 garlic clove, crushed
1 sprig of fresh thyme	50 g (2 oz) Braised Lentils (see p. 80)
1 bay leaf	1 tablespoon chopped fresh parsley
About 1.75–2.25 litres (3–4 pints) Chicken Stock (see p. 228)	Salt and freshly ground black pepper
	1 quantity Mashed Potatoes (see p. 142)

Soak the bacon in water for 24 hours before cooking. This will reduce the salt content.

Put the bacon in a large pot. Coarsely chop two of the carrots, one of the onions, the celery and leek and add to the pot with the herbs. Cover with chicken stock, bring to the simmer, skim off any impurities, cover and cook gently for about 1½ hours until cooked. Allow to rest for 30 minutes in the stock.

Cook the pearl barley in some of the cooking liquor for about 15–20 minutes until soft. Cut the remaining vegetables into 1 cm (½ in) dice and sweat in half the butter with the garlic. Add the pearl barley and a little more stock, if necessary, to give a soup consistency. Allow this to simmer for about 15 minutes until all the vegetables are tender. Add the cooked lentils, the remaining knobs of butter and the chopped parsley to create a barley, lentil and vegetable stew. Check for seasoning.

To serve, sit the warm mashed potatoes in the centre of the serving plates and spoon some of the stew around. Slice the bacon, allow two slices per portion, and place on the potatoes. Finish with a spoonful of stock on top of the meat and serve.

Jellied Bacon with Parsley

This is a very tasty, traditional English dish. It can simply be spooned on to a plate and served with lettuce leaves and a potato salad, the recipe for which is to be found on p. 141.

SERVES 4

1.8 kg (4 lb) unsmoked bacon collar	6 shallots or 3 onions, finely chopped
2 carrots	150 ml (5 fl oz) dry white wine
1 onion	150 ml (5 fl oz) white wine vinegar
2 celery sticks	2 teaspoons chopped fresh parsley
1 leek	
1 bay leaf	Salt and freshly ground black pepper
1.2–1.75 litres (2–3 pints) Chicken Stock (see p. 228)	

Cooking the bacon is best done either in the morning or the day before. Put the bacon, carrots, onion, celery, leek, bay leaf and chicken stock in a pan, making sure the stock covers the meat. Bring to the simmer, cover and simmer gently for 1 hour until the bacon is cooked. Allow the bacon to cool in the stock then transfer it to a clean container. Pass the cooking liquor through a fine sieve; it will set to a jelly.

While the stock is setting, cover the chopped shallots with the white wine and wine vinegar in a small pan. Boil to reduce until dry then leave to cool.

Taste the jelly, and if it is a little bland, it may now need to be re-boiled and reduced for a stronger taste. When it is ready, sit it on a bowl of ice and allow it to cool almost to setting point. It will have almost jellied.

Trim the bacon of any excess fat; the meat will be nice and moist. Slice and shred the bacon into thin strips and mix with the parsley and shallots. Check for seasoning and add the stock. Pour the mix into a bowl or tray and chill in the fridge until set.

OPPOSITE
Jellied Bacon with Parsley
served with New Potato Salad
(see p. 141).

Home-made Pork Sausages

There are so many varieties of sausage available in the shops, good ones, too, that you're probably wondering why I'm making my own. Well, they've become a Great British Classic, and I like making classic dishes. They give me a great sense of achievement and taste really good too (see p. 119)!

If you do decide to make the sausages, speak to your butcher a day or two before and order the pigs' cheeks and sausage skins. The cheeks are totally fat free and have great flavour; you need just the centre, meaty part. Also make sure the shoulder is boned and rindless. You can make life even easier, however, by replacing the shoulder, cheeks and back fat with trimmed pork belly. I like to serve the sausages with Split Pea Fritters (see opposite), arranging two sausages on top of each fritter. I also like to serve them with an Onion Gravy (see p. 233) which you may well want to pass through a sieve for a smoother sauce.

MAKES about 16 sausages

900 g (2 lb) boned and rinded shoulder of pork	Salt and freshly ground black pepper
4 pigs' cheeks, trimmed	A pinch of ground mace
225 g (8 oz) rinded pork back fat	2 slices white bread, crusts removed and crumbed
2 onions, very finely chopped	1 egg, beaten
25 g (1 oz) unsalted butter	Worcestershire sauce
¼ teaspoon chopped fresh thyme	About 4 metres (4½ yards) sausage skins, soaked in cold water
¼ teaspoon chopped fresh sage	50 g (2 oz) lard
1 garlic clove, crushed	

Mince the shoulder, cheeks and back fat through a medium mincer. I like to keep the mix fairly coarse and only mince the meat once. If you prefer a smoother texture then mince once more.

Sweat the chopped onions in the butter with the herbs and garlic for 2–3 minutes until soft. If there is any excess liquid once the onions are cooked, turn up the heat and boil to reduce until dry. Leave to cool. When the onions are cold, mix them with the pork meat and season with salt, pepper and ground mace. Add the breadcrumbs and egg. A few drops of Worcestershire sauce will now finish the taste.

The skins will have been preserved in salt and will need to be well soaked and rinsed in cold water. Cut the skin into sixteen 25 cm (10 in) lengths and tie a knot in one end. Fill a piping bag with the sausage meat and pipe into the skin. Fill to the size of a standard pork sausage, then tie a knot in the other end. This will leave 5–8 cm (2–3 in) of spare sausage skin which will shrink during cooking. Repeat the process with the remaining sausage mix. Rest the sausages in the fridge for 30 minutes.

The sausages are now ready to cook. They must be treated carefully during cooking and not fried on a high heat. Melt the lard and cook the sausages over a medium heat for about 10 minutes until browned on all sides. The sausages are now ready to eat. They can be simply placed on top of the pea fritters and the onion sauce poured around, or even just eaten in a roll!

Split Pea Fritters

SERVES 4

100 g (4 oz) plain flour
A pinch of salt
1 egg
300 ml (10 fl oz) milk
1 tablespoon unsalted butter, melted

1 teaspoon chopped fresh parsley
8 tablespoons Braised Split Peas
(see p. 154)
Salt and freshly ground white pepper
2 tablespoons vegetable oil

Sieve the flour and salt into a bowl. Beat the egg with half the milk then fold the mixture into the flour. Gradually add more of the milk until the mixture is thick enough to coat the back of a spoon. Add the melted butter and chopped parsley.

The split peas must be cold. Slowly fold some of the batter into the peas until you have a thick pancake mix; not all the batter may be needed. Season with salt and pepper.

Heat a little oil in a 15 cm (6 in) pancake pan and pour in the batter to about 6 mm (¼ in) thick. Fry until golden brown, then turn over in the pan and fry the other side. Keep warm while you make three more fritters.

66 *The simplest cooking techniques are still the best.* **99**

Barbecuing chicken breasts to serve with Noodles in Creamy Mushroom Sauce (see p. 92), Home-made Pork Sausages (see p. 116) and Split Pea Fritters (see p. 117).

Fillet of Venison Wellington

This dish is usually associated with fillet of beef, but I've tried it with venison, added some chestnuts to the stuffing, and served it with a slightly sweetened sauce and found it really delicious. You can, of course, follow this recipe for fillet of beef but omit the chestnuts and cook for an extra 20 minutes. Two dishes from one recipe! Ask your butcher to bone the venison for you and trim the fillet of all sinew. Take the bones home to add flavour to the sauce.

Another way to serve this is to make the Bubble and Squeak on p. 147, either cooked as per the recipe or in individual cakes. The venison slices can then be placed on top of the cakes and the sauce poured around.

SERVES 4

1 × 450–750 g (1–1½ lb) boned loin of venison from a saddle of fallow deer
275 g (10 oz) Puff Pastry (see p. 216)
50 g (2 oz) unsalted butter

Salt and freshly ground white pepper
4–6 thin Savoury Pancakes (see p. 208)
1 egg, beaten

For the Stuffing

225 g (8 oz) mushrooms, minced or finely chopped
1 onion, finely chopped
2 smoked back bacon rashers, rinded and finely diced
1 garlic clove, crushed
A pinch of chopped fresh sage
A pinch of chopped fresh thyme

25 g (1 oz) unsalted butter
50 g (2 oz) shelled chestnuts, chopped
25 g (1 oz) fresh white breadcrumbs
1 teaspoon chopped fresh parsley
1 large chicken breast, skinned and minced or very finely chopped
Salt and freshly ground white pepper
1 egg, beaten

For the Sauce

Venison bones (optional)
600 ml (1 pint) Red Wine Sauce (see p. 236)
1–2 teaspoons cranberry jelly

To make the stuffing, cook the mushrooms on their own in a pan until almost dry. Cook the chopped onion, bacon, garlic, sage and thyme in the butter for a few minutes without colouring. Leave to cool. Add the chestnuts, breadcrumbs and parsley. Season the chicken with salt and pepper, gradually mix in the egg and mix until firm to the touch. Stir in the mushrooms and the onion mixture and check for seasoning.

The sauce can be made in advance. If you have the venison bones, pre-heat the oven to 220°C/425°F/gas 7. Chop the bones and roast in the pre-heated oven for about 30 minutes until browned. Add them to the reduction for the red wine sauce (see p. 236) before adding the veal *jus*, then cook in the normal way. Once the sauce has been pushed through a sieve a good venison flavour will have developed. Stir in the cranberry jelly to give a slightly sweeter taste.

Roll out the pastry until large enough to wrap the venison; the thinnest should be 3 mm (⅛ in) and the absolute thickest is 5 mm (¼ in). Leave to rest in the fridge.

Season the venison and fry in the butter in a hot pan until coloured on all sides but not cooked. Leave to cool.

To make the Wellington, lay two of the pancakes on the centre of the pastry and spread some of the stuffing over to cover them. Lay the meat on top and spread some more of the stuffing on top. Fold the pancakes around the meat and lay the other two on top. Brush the edges of the pastry with beaten egg and fold over to enclose the meat and stuffing. Trim off any excess pastry and turn the parcel over on to a dampened roasting tray. Leave to rest in the fridge for 30 minutes.

Pre-heat the oven to 220°C/425°F/gas 7.

Brush the pastry with a little more beaten egg. The pastry can be decorated with pastry trimmings or left plain. Roast in the pre-heated oven for 20–25 minutes. This will leave the meat still pink inside. Leave to rest for 10–15 minutes.

Slice the Wellington, allowing three slices per portion, and serve with the hot, rich sauce.

Steak and Kidney Pudding

There are many recipes for steak and kidney puddings. This one is a little more involved, but I think gets the best results (see pp. 126–7). It's best to have some fresh and some dried suet, but if not you can use just the dried.

SERVES 6–8

900 g (2 lb) braising steak, trimmed and
   cut into 2.5 cm (1 in) dice
450 g (1 lb) ox or lambs' kidneys,
   trimmed and cut into 2.5 cm
   (1 in) dice
50–75 g (2–3 oz) beef dripping
6 celery sticks, diced
6 carrots, diced
8 onions, diced

225 g (8 oz) mushrooms, quartered
   (optional)
1 garlic clove, crushed
½ teaspoon chopped fresh thyme
50 g (2 oz) unsalted butter
300 ml (10 fl oz) Guinness
1.75 litres (3 pints) Veal *Jus* (see p. 232)
   or bought alternative (see p. 225)
Salt and freshly ground white pepper

For the Suet Paste

450 g (1 lb) plain flour
25 g (1 oz) baking powder
100 g (4 oz) fresh suet, chopped
100 g (4 oz) dried suet
300 ml (10 fl oz) water

Grease two 1.2 litre (2 pint) pudding basins or six 400 ml (14 fl oz) moulds.

For the steak and kidney filling, fry the beef and kidney in the dripping, allowing it to colour well on all sides.

In a separate large pan, sweat the diced vegetables and mushrooms, if using, garlic and herbs in the butter for a few minutes until soft. Add the Guinness and boil to reduce until almost dry. Add the meat and cover with the *jus*. Bring to the simmer, cover, and simmer for 1–1½ hours until the meat is tender. Check the seasoning and allow to cool.

While the meat is cooking, make the suet paste. Sieve the flour, baking powder and a pinch of salt into a bowl. Mix in the suets then fold in the water to form a fairly firm paste. Allow the paste to rest for about 20 minutes. Roll out the paste and use the majority to line the pudding moulds; you will need some left for the lids. Keep in the fridge until needed.

When the filling is cold, fill the moulds with the meat mixture, using a slotted spoon. You need only a little liquid in the filling. Roll out the remaining suet paste and cover the moulds, trim and press together. Top with pieces of buttered foil.

Stand the puddings in a steamer or a pan half-filled with hot water, cover and steam for about 1 hour for the smaller puddings and 1½–2 hours for the larger ones, topping up with boiling water as necessary.

The liquid left from the stew can be re-boiled, pushed through a sieve and used as the gravy.

To serve, trim round the tops. Turn the individual puddings out on to hot plates and cover with the gravy. From the larger basins, cut and spoon on to hot plates and cover with gravy.

Beef Olives with Black Pudding

The stuffing for the beef olives is made from the same base as for the Jambonette de Volaille (see p. 96), using onions, mushrooms, garlic and herbs. The black pudding works very well in the recipe, and can be broken down with a wooden spoon if mincing is impossible. The beef olives can be served plain or some garnish can be added. I've chosen the button onions, mushrooms and bacon to give extra flavours and texture to the dish.

SERVES 4

700 g (1½ lb) lean beef topside or rump
Salt and freshly ground white pepper
225 g (8 oz) pig's caul, soaked in cold
   water for 24 hours (optional,
   see method)

1.2 litres (2 pints) Red Wine Sauce
   (see p. 236) or Veal *Jus* (see p. 232)
50 g (2 oz) beef dripping

For the Stuffing

225 g (8 oz) black pudding, skinned and
   minced
1 chicken breast, minced or finely
   chopped
1 egg
3 onions, finely chopped
2 garlic cloves, crushed

A few fresh sage leaves, chopped
½ teaspoon chopped fresh thyme
50 g (2 oz) unsalted butter
175 g (6 oz) button mushrooms, minced
   and cooked until dry

For the Garnish

100 g (4 oz) button onions
100 g (4 oz) unsalted butter
100 g (4 oz) bacon, rinded and diced
100 g (4 oz) button mushrooms
2 teaspoons chopped fresh parsley

To make the stuffing, mix together the black pudding and chicken breast, season with salt and pepper and add the egg. Fry the chopped onions, garlic and herbs in the butter until softened, then allow to cool. Cook the mushrooms in a separate pan until dry then leave to cool. When cold, mix all the ingredients and beat together well. Check for seasoning and adjust to taste with salt and pepper.

Cut the meat into eight thin slices and sit each slice between two sheets of cling film. These can now be batted with a rolling pin to stretch the meat. Divide the filling between the slices then roll them up, folding in the sides to form a cylindrical beef olive shape. Wrap them individually in the pig's caul, if using, to keep the shape of the meat, or pierce and hold them in shape with cocktail sticks.

Start to warm the red wine sauce or *jus* in a large, lidded braising pan, making sure the sauce is not too thick; when the olives are slowly cooking in the sauce, it will thicken.

Fry the beef olives in the dripping for a few minutes until well coloured on all sides. Drain off any excess fat and sit the beef olives in the red wine sauce or gravy. Bring to the simmer and cook gently for about 1½ hours. Check the meat: it should start to feel soft and give when pinched. Simmer for a further 30 minutes, then the olives will be tender and ready.

Drain the sauce into a pan and re-boil, skimming off any excess fat or impurities if necessary. Return the beef olives to the sauce to warm through.

To make the garnish, fry the onions in butter until soft and golden brown. Remove from the pan and add the bacon and mushrooms. These can be fried together on top of the stove until the bacon is brown and crispy. Add the garnishes to the sauce.

To serve, remove the cocktail sticks, if using, from the beef olives, and serve the olives into hot bowls, allowing two per portion. Spoon the garnish and sauce over and sprinkle with the chopped parsley.

OVERLEAF
Four classic dishes: top left, Steak and Kidney Pudding (see p. 122), top right, Irish Stew (see p. 129), below left, Beef Stew and Dumplings (see p. 128) and below right, Home-made Lamb Pasties (see p. 134).

Beef Stew and Dumplings

This is a classic British dish which is a total meal in itself (see previous page). You've got the meat, the vegetables and the dumplings all in one dish. The chestnuts are optional but I really enjoy the nutty taste they give the dish.

SERVES 4–6

900 g (2 lb) braising steak, trimmed and
    cut into 2.5 cm (1 in) dice
Salt and freshly ground black pepper
100 g (4 oz) beef dripping
4 large onions, diced
1 garlic clove, crushed
1 sprig of fresh thyme
25 g (1 oz) unsalted butter

½ bottle red wine
1.75 litres (3 pints) Veal *Jus* (see p. 232)
    or bought alternative (see p. 225)
6 carrots
6 celery sticks
4 large potatoes, peeled
350 g (12 oz) button mushrooms
1 tablespoon tomato purée (optional)

For the Dumplings

1 onion, finely chopped
4 smoked back bacon rashers, rinded
    and diced
1 teaspoon chopped fresh thyme
25 g (1 oz) unsalted butter
100 g (4 oz) chestnuts, cooked, shelled
    and chopped (optional)

225 g (8 oz) plain flour
2 teaspoons baking powder
100 g (4 oz) fresh or dried beef suet,
    shredded
150 ml (5 fl oz) water
Chicken Stock (see p. 228)
    or water

Season the meat with salt and pepper and fry in the beef dripping until brown. Leave to drain in a colander. Meanwhile, in a large flameproof casserole, sweat the diced onions, garlic and thyme in the butter for a few minutes until soft. Add the red wine and boil until reduced by two-thirds. Add the *jus*, bring to the boil, and add the steak. Cover and leave to simmer gently for 1½ hours.

Cut the carrots, celery and potatoes into large dice and add them to the stew with the whole button mushrooms and tomato purée. Continue to cook for another 15–20 minutes until the vegetables are soft. Check for seasoning.

Meanwhile, make the dumplings. Sweat the chopped onion, bacon and thyme in the butter until soft. Add the chopped chestnuts, if using, then allow the mixture to cool.

Mix together the flour, baking powder and suet. Add a pinch of salt and the onion mixture and mix to a dough with the water. The dumplings can now be rolled into balls 2.5–4 cm (1–1½ in) in diameter. Bring the chicken stock or water to the boil, add the dumplings and simmer for 20 minutes. Serve the stew in hot bowls, and to finish top with the dumplings.

Irish Stew

This dish can be prepared and cooked in many different ways. You can look in a dozen cookery books and you'll find a dozen varying recipes. Well, this is my version (see pp. 126–7).

SERVES 4

750 g (1½ lb) middle neck of lamb, cut into cutlets
100 g (4 oz) unsalted butter
4 onions, sliced
450 g (1 lb) potatoes, peeled and cut into 2.5 cm (1 in) dice
1 garlic clove
1 bouquet garni (1 bay leaf, 1 sprig each of fresh rosemary and thyme tied in a square of muslin or strip of leek) or bouquet garni sachet

1.5 litres (2½ pints) Chicken Stock (see p. 228) or water
175 g (6 oz) carrots, diced
6 celery sticks, cut into 2.5 cm (1 in) dice
225 g (8 oz) Savoy cabbage, shredded
Salt and freshly ground white pepper
2 teaspoons chopped fresh parsley

Cover the meat with cold water in a large pan and bring to the boil. Drain off the water and refresh the meat in cold water. Drain well.

Melt the butter in a large braising pan and add the sliced onions, half the diced potatoes and the garlic. Add the bouquet garni to the pan and sweat for 2 minutes. Add the lamb cutlets and cover with the chicken stock. Bring the stock to the simmer, cover and cook for 30 minutes. The meat will be half-cooked and the potatoes will have started to purée and thicken the stock. Add the diced carrots and continue to cook for a further 10 minutes. Add the remaining potatoes and the diced celery and cook for 15–20 minutes. At this stage we do not want to purée the potatoes but just cook them until soft. Add the cabbage and cook for another 2–3 minutes until the meat and vegetables are tender. Season with salt and pepper, remove the bouquet garni and serve in individual bowls or one large bowl. Finish with the chopped parsley. You now have a complete meal.

*My own version of
a traditional
Lancashire Hot-pot
(see p. 132).*

Lancashire Hot-pot

This is a Great British Classic. It's usually just neck of lamb, kidneys, onions, potatoes and gravy, but I've tried to refine it, by adding more textures and tastes. It also looks a lot nicer when presented, and just shows how good ordinary lamb chump chops can be (see previous page). The chops should be lean with the little bone and fat left on. The vegetables have to be chopped into very small dice, which may sound tiresome but it's worth doing. You will need a shallow flameproof braising dish to hold the chops in one layer.

SERVES 4

2 carrots, finely diced
2 celery sticks, finely diced
2 onions, finely diced
1 leek, finely diced
50–75 g (2–3 oz) unsalted butter
½ garlic clove, crushed
2 large sprigs of fresh rosemary
4 thick, lean lamb chump chops

150 ml (5 fl oz) dry white wine
900 ml (1½ pints) Veal *Jus* (see p. 232)
   or bought alternative (see p. 225)
4 large potatoes, peeled
1 tablespoon lamb fat or beef dripping
Salt and freshly ground white pepper
A sprinkling of chopped fresh
   parsley

Pre-heat the oven to 200°C/400°F/gas 6.

Lightly cook the diced vegetables in the butter with the garlic and rosemary for a few minutes until softened. Drain and keep to one side. Fry the chops in the butter remaining in the pan for about 3–4 minutes on each side until golden. Remove and drain. Add the white wine to the pan and boil to reduce until almost dry. This will help release all the flavours into the sauce. Add the *jus*, bring just to the boil, then strain through a sieve.

Shape the potatoes into cylinders and slice them 3 mm (⅛ in) thick. You will need about ten slices per chop. Fry the potatoes in the fat or dripping until golden, then drain well.

Place the chops in the braising dish and spoon the vegetables on top, covering all the lamb. Season with salt and pepper. Layer the potatoes on top of the vegetables, overlapping them almost to resemble fish scales. Pour the gravy around and bring to the simmer. Place in the pre-heated oven and allow to braise for about 40–45 minutes. The potatoes should be crisp and golden.

Remove the chops with the vegetables and potatoes still on top. Bring the sauce to the boil, skimming off any impurities. It should be rich and dark, just thick enough to coat the back of a spoon. Place the chops in hot bowls, pour the sauce around and sprinkle with chopped parsley.

Chump of Lamb
Marinated with Red Wine and Orange

There are many ways of cooking and serving this dish. The lamb cooks beautifully on a barbecue grill, leaving it nicely burnt outside and still pink in the centre. This gives a lovely bitter-sweet taste that will eat well with a mixed or green salad. But for this recipe, I'm going to roast the lamb and make a sauce with the marinade.

Lamb chumps are taken from the saddle of lamb towards the tail end. They can be cut into chump chops or left as one piece, rolled and tied. For this recipe they are going to be just that, like individual roasts. One of my favourite dishes to go with this is Buttered Spetzli with Leeks (see p. 155).

SERVES 4

4 chumps of lamb, each about 225–275 g (8–10 oz), rolled and tied

25 g (1 oz) lard

600 ml (1 pint) Veal *Jus* (see p. 232) or bought alternative (see p. 225) (optional)

For the Marinade

½ bottle red wine

2 shallots or 1 onion, chopped

2 garlic cloves, sliced

Zest of 1 orange

1 sprig of fresh thyme

1 sprig of fresh rosemary

1 sprig of fresh tarragon

A few black peppercorns, crushed

Mix all the marinade ingredients together in a dish large enough to hold the chumps in one layer. Add the chump roasts, cover and leave to marinate. The flavour gets better if left longer. I prefer to marinate in the fridge for up to 5 days for the best results. You will find that the lamb is now deep red in colour.

Pre-heat the oven to 220°C/425°F/gas 7. Pre-heat a roasting tray and fry the chumps in the lard on top of the stove until almost burnt and crisp. Then place the tray in the pre-heated oven and roast for 15–20 minutes. Remove from the oven and leave to rest for 6–8 minutes.

While the lamb is roasting, boil the marinade until reduced by three-quarters. Add the *jus*, if using, then leave to simmer for 15 minutes. Pass the sauce through a sieve.

The lamb chumps can now be sliced and served with the sauce.

Home-made Lamb Pasties

This is not a Cornish pasty recipe – or at least so I've been told – so I've changed its name to 'home-made' (see pp. 126–7). It's my version of a pasty – light, crisp and very tasty. If you do not have time to make your own pastry, you can use a shop-bought puff or flaky pastry. Should you have any filling left over, this will keep in the fridge and can be eaten just as mince or made into a shepherd's pie.

MAKES 8 pasties

750 g (1½ lb) Puff Pastry (see p. 216)
1 egg, beaten

For the Filling

450 g (1 lb) lean lamb, coarsely minced
   or chopped
25 g (1 oz) beef dripping or lamb fat
1 garlic clove, crushed
½ teaspoon chopped fresh thyme
½ teaspoon chopped fresh sage
100 g (4 oz) onions, cut into 1 cm
   (½ in) dice
100 g (4 oz) carrots, cut into 1 cm
   (½ in) dice
100 g (4 oz) celery, cut into 1 cm
   (½ in) dice
Salt and freshly ground white pepper

25 g (1 oz) plain flour
900 ml (1½ pints) Chicken Stock (see
   p. 228) reduced to 300 ml (10 fl oz)
100 g (4 oz) swede, cut into 1 cm
   (½ in) dice
100 g (4 oz) parsnip, cut into 1 cm
   (½ in) dice
600 ml (1 pint) Veal *Jus* (see p. 232) or
   bought alternative (see p. 225)
   (150 ml (5 fl oz) for mixture and
   optional 450 ml (15 fl oz) for gravy)
2 potatoes, cooked in their skins
Worcestershire sauce

Fry the minced lamb in the dripping, colouring on all sides and separating the grains. Add the garlic, herbs, diced onions, carrots and celery, cover and cook for about 10 minutes. Season with salt and generously with pepper. Add the flour and continue to cook for a few minutes. Add one-third of the reduced chicken stock and cook for 10–15 minutes. Add the parsnips and swedes and another one-third of the stock and cook for 10 minutes. Check for seasoning and add the remaining stock and 150 ml (5 fl oz) of veal *jus*.

Peel the boiled potatoes and cut into 1 cm (½ in) dice. Add them to the meat and cook for 5–6 minutes. Check for seasoning with salt and pepper once again, and add 2–3 drops of Worcestershire sauce for an extra spicy flavour. Allow the mix to cool.

Roll out the puff pastry and cut into six to eight 15 cm (6 in) squares. When the filling mix is cold, spoon some on to each square of pastry slightly off-centre. Brush around the edges with the beaten egg and fold over diagonally to make a triangle. Trim to a semi-circle, shape and then pinch with thumb and forefinger all the way round the edges to seal. Brush over each of the pasties with beaten egg and leave in the fridge for about 20 minutes before baking.

Pre-heat the oven to 200°C/400°F/gas 6 and dampen a baking sheet.

To cook the pasties, just sit them on the prepared baking sheet and bake in the pre-heated oven for about 30 minutes. They should be crisp and golden brown. These can now be eaten as they are or served with the remaining hot *jus*.

Roast Fillets of Lamb on Aubergine with Provençale Onions

The best end of lamb is positioned between the saddle of lamb and the middle neck. It is one of the most popular cuts of lamb. At most butchers they are sold 'French trimmed', which means they are cut and cleaned to show the individual bones – the best way to buy them. You can cook them as racks of lamb or cut them into individual lamb cutlets. Another alternative is to remove the meat from the bones so that you are left with two fillets, which is what you want here. These can now be halved to give you four portions. The fat will just tear off leaving the meat clean.

2 small aubergines
Salt and freshly ground black pepper
25 g (1 oz) beef dripping or lamb fat
2 best ends of lamb, boned

2 tablespoons olive oil
450 ml (15 fl oz) Tomato and Onion
    Flavoured Gravy (see p. 239)

For the Provençale Onions

2 tablespoons olive oil
2 large onions, finely chopped
2 garlic cloves, crushed
½ bunch of fresh basil, chopped
½ bunch of fresh tarragon, chopped

450 g (1 lb) button mushrooms,
    sliced
300 ml (10 fl oz) dry white wine
150 ml (5 fl oz) Tomato Coulis (see
    p. 240) or 2 teaspoons tomato purée

Pre-heat the oven to 220°C/425°F/gas 7.

Slice the aubergines into six pieces each, sprinkle with some salt and leave them to drain in a colander for about 30 minutes.

To make the Provençale onions, heat the olive oil in a pan and add the chopped onions and garlic. Cover with a lid and cook over a low heat for 5 minutes. Remove the lid and add the chopped herbs and sliced mushrooms. Continue to cook for 5–6 minutes. Add the white wine, increase the heat and boil to reduce until almost dry. Add the tomato coulis or purée and bring to the simmer. Season with salt and pepper. The sauce should be fairly thick. Keep the sauce warm.

Pre-heat a small roasting tray and add the dripping or fat. Season the lamb with salt and pepper and fry in the fat until coloured on all sides, then put the lamb in the pre-heated oven and roast for about 10–12 minutes. After this cooking time, the meat will just give when pressed between thumb and forefinger; at this stage it will be medium rare to medium. Remove the lamb from the oven and leave to rest in a warm place for 10 minutes before slicing.

While the lamb is resting, lightly rinse the salt from the aubergines and dry on a cloth. Heat the olive oil in a frying-pan and cook the aubergines until golden on both sides. Drain well on kitchen paper. Heat the tomato and onion gravy through gently.

Lay the aubergine slices on to hot plates, three slices per portion, and spoon the Provençale onions on top. Carve the lamb lengthways, allowing five to six slices per fillet. Overlap the slices on the onions and pour the tomato and onion gravy around.

Vegetarian and Vegetable Dishes

Vegetables in British cooking tend to be seen and used as side dishes, as an accompaniment to a roast or stewed meat or chicken. On the Continent, they're regarded as dishes in their own right, and I think we should all start to look at serving and eating them in that way, too; they're as important as all the rest.

A lot of the recipes here and throughout the book are fairly versatile. For instance, the Stuffed Tomatoes with Fried Leeks are a popular vegetarian main course, but could quite easily be made individually as a vegetable side dish or served as a starter. And some of the recipes listed in the Starters section could serve as vegetarian main courses: the Gruyère Cheese Flan, Spanish Omelette or Grilled Aubergines. Likewise the Spinach Dumplings or Potato Raviolis here can make good starters. In fact, there's another recipe which could be both a starter or a main course, and was something I was often given at tea time when I was a child: Macaroni Cheese. My version has been enhanced by leeks and onions, which give a whole new flavour.

All any vegetable needs to make it delicious and healthy is a little care and attention. If you're cooking green vegetables like peas or green beans, then make sure that you cook them in plenty of boiling salted water, lid off, for a few minutes only. If you're serving them there and then, just drain, toss in butter and season with salt and pepper. But some vegetables can be thought about much earlier. When you're having a dinner party, you can prepare and part-cook some vegetables in the morning. If you have a microwave, you can cook, butter, season and chill them in the morning, then simply heat and serve them in the evening! If you are without a microwave, Glazed Carrots can be simply tossed in butter to re-heat, as can the individual ingredients for the Cabbage, Celeriac and Carrot dish; just mix together when cold then re-heat. This really saves you spending all evening in the kitchen although, obviously any of the roasted vegetables, like celeriac or parsnip, would have to be cooked at the last minute to keep them crisp.

The potato is a Great British vegetable, and there are so many ways in which to prepare it. Bubble and Squeak and Colcannon are very similar in terms of raw ingredients, but in fact are cooked and served very differently. I always associate Bubble and Squeak with left-overs, whereas Colcannon is a completely separate dish of potato, spring onion and cabbage, served almost as creamed potatoes.

Talking of creamed potatoes, that really has to be my favourite of all potato dishes – boiled potatoes, mashed with butter and milk or cream. But it isn't always all that easy to make: the potatoes have to be right (a good Maris Piper always works); they mustn't be too over-cooked, or too over-worked. Perfection will do! With a good mashing, after the cream or milk and butter are added, season with salt, pepper and a pinch of nutmeg; they will finish creamily smooth with a good texture and lovely potato flavour. You'll see what I mean when I say they're my favourite; I use them in quite a few main course dishes!

So, a few golden rules for vegetables are:

1 Buy them fresh.
2 Cook them simply.
3 Always eat plenty of them!

OPPOSITE
All any vegetable needs
to make it delicious and
healthy is a little care
and attention.

Potato Raviolis
with Mushroom and Stilton

This is a ravioli with a difference: the 'pasta' is actually made with mashed potato. The mixture rolls as easily as pastry, and fries to a crisp golden brown. This works well as a main course or a starter and can be served as a vegetarian dish.

SERVES 4–6

For the Ravioli

350 g (12 oz) Mashed Potatoes without cream or butter (see p. 142)

2 egg yolks

2 tablespoons olive oil

Salt and freshly ground white pepper

3 tablespoons plain flour

For the Filling and Sauce

1 onion, finely chopped

1 sprig of fresh thyme

2 garlic cloves, crushed

25 g (1 oz) unsalted butter

100 g (4 oz) button mushrooms, quartered

100 g (4 oz) mixed wild mushrooms, or 225 g (8 oz) button mushrooms if unavailable

300 ml (10 fl oz) dry white wine

150 ml (5 fl oz) Vegetable or Chicken Stock (see pp. 229 or 228)

150 ml (5 fl oz) double cream

100 g (4 oz) Stilton, grated or crumbled

To Cook and Garnish

25 g (1 oz) unsalted butter

50 g (2 oz) mixed wild mushrooms or sliced button mushrooms

50 ml (2 fl oz) olive oil

Juice of ½ lemon

½ teaspoon chopped fresh parsley

To make the ravioli paste, while the mashed potatoes are still warm, add the egg yolks and olive oil, season with salt and pepper and fold in the flour. This will now have a pasta paste texture. Cover with cling film and keep warm.

To make the filling, cook the chopped onion, thyme and garlic in the butter for 5 minutes. Add the mushrooms and cook for a further 5 minutes. Add the white wine and boil to reduce by half. Add the chicken or vegetable stock and simmer for a further 5 minutes. Add the cream and continue to cook gently for a further 10 minutes. Season with salt and pepper and strain off three-quarters of the liquid, which will be the sauce. Leave to one side.

Warm the remaining filling and add the Stilton. Melt this into the mixture then spread it on to a tray to cool. When cool, place in the fridge for 10–15 minutes until set.

Divide the ravioli paste into four or six pieces and roll out into circles (about the same thickness as pastry) on a lightly floured board. Spoon the mushroom filling on to one half of each ravioli circle and fold the other half over, pressing down all round the edges. The raviolis can now be shaped with a round pastry cutter to make a neater semi-circle. If the raviolis are made a few hours before eating, sit them on a tray sprinkled liberally with semolina to prevent them sticking.

To cook, melt the butter in a frying-pan and fry the raviolis for 3–4 minutes on each side until golden. Remove them from the pan. While the raviolis are frying, sauté the sliced mushrooms in the butter and a teaspoon of the olive oil. Season with salt and pepper.

Warm the cream sauce and pour it into four bowls. Sit the raviolis on the sauce and spoon the garnishing mushrooms on top. Mix the remaining garnish olive oil with the lemon juice, some salt, pepper and chopped parsley and spoon over the mushrooms.

New Potato Salad

SERVES 4

900 g (2 lb) new potatoes

1 large onion, finely chopped
4–5 tablespoons Basic Vinaigrette
(see p. 245)
Salt and freshly ground black pepper
300 ml (10 fl oz) Mayonnaise (see p. 248)

Boil the potatoes until cooked. While still hot, cut into quarters and place in a bowl. Add the onion and sprinkle with vinaigrette to taste. Season with salt and pepper. While the potatoes are cooling, they will absorb the vinaigrette, which will help the taste. When cold, bind with the mayonnaise to finish.

Colcannon

This is lovely as a totally vegetarian dish – perhaps with a poached egg on top – or a great accompaniment for Boiled Bacon (see p. 113) with a parsley sauce or Home-made Pork Sausages with Onion Gravy (see p. 116). You can use kale, or white or green cabbage.

SERVES 4

450 g (1 lb) potatoes, peeled
450 g (1 lb) kale or cabbage, shredded
2 small leeks or spring onion tops,
   chopped

150 g (5 oz) unsalted butter
Salt and freshly ground black pepper
A pinch of ground mace
150 ml (5 fl oz) milk or single cream

Boil the potatoes in salted water until cooked, about 20–25 minutes depending on size. Drain off all the water and replace the lid. Shake the pan vigorously which will start to break the potatoes, then mash them until light and fluffy. Blanch the shredded kale or cabbage in boiling water for 2–3 minutes until softened but not coloured. Drain well. Fry the chopped leeks or spring onion tops in 25 g (1 oz) of the butter for a few minutes until softened, then add the cabbage and continue to cook for a few more minutes. Add the potatoes with the salt, pepper, ground mace and milk or cream. Melt the remaining butter and add it to the mix. Heat through, check for seasoning with salt and pepper, and serve.

Mashed Potatoes

Mashed potatoes are looked upon as a simple, straightforward dish, with any old potato being used for the recipe. I think very differently. During the seasons, various potatoes are available, but I have always found that Maris Piper are easily obtained and purée very well. The rest, of course, is taking care in the cooking and finishing of the dish.

SERVES 4–6

900 g (2 lb) potatoes, peeled and
   quartered
Salt and freshly ground white pepper

100 g (4 oz) unsalted butter
120 ml (4 fl oz) double cream or milk
Freshly grated nutmeg

Boil the potatoes in salted water until cooked, about 20–25 minutes depending on size. Drain off all the water and replace the lid. Shake the pan vigorously which will start to break the potatoes. Add the butter and cream or milk a little at a time, while mashing the potatoes. Season with salt, pepper and nutmeg. The potatoes will now be light, fluffy, creamy and ready to eat.

Variation

Many different flavours can now be added for any particular dish. About 50–85 ml (2–3 fl oz) of olive oil can replace the butter, or 1–2 tablespoons of Pesto Sauce (see p. 243) can be added for a different taste. To the basic mashed potato recipe, I sometimes like to add the juice of 1 lemon and 1–2 tablespoons of finely chopped raw shallot. This works really well with fish, especially the Soused Mackerel on p. 41.

Potato and Leek Gratin

This beautifully creamy, tasty potato dish goes very well with most of my main courses.

SERVES 4

450 g (1 lb) leeks
2 onions, sliced
25 g (1 oz) unsalted butter
600 ml (1 pint) double cream
450 g (1 lb) potatoes, peeled and thinly sliced

1 small garlic clove, crushed
Salt and freshly ground white pepper
Freshly grated nutmeg
50 g (2 oz) Cheddar, grated (optional)

Pre-heat the oven to 180°C/350°F/gas 4 and grease a shallow ovenproof gratin dish.

Cut the leeks diagonally into 5 mm (¼ in) slices and blanch in boiling water for 30 seconds. Drain, rinse under cold water, drain again and pat dry.

Cook the onions in the butter for 2–3 minutes until softened.

Pour the cream over the sliced potatoes in a pan. Add the garlic and season with salt, pepper and nutmeg. Bring to the boil then stir in the leeks and onions. Pour the mixture into the prepared dish to a depth of 4 cm (1½ in), covering with all the cream. Place the dish into a roasting tray filled with very hot water and bake in the pre-heated oven for 1 hour until the potatoes are cooked through and golden brown on top. To check the potatoes during cooking, just pierce with a small vegetable knife. When it goes through easily you will know they are cooked.

Remove the dish from the hot water. As a finish you can top with the grated Cheddar and glaze under a hot grill until golden brown.

Macaroni Cheese with Leeks and Onions

We all know macaroni cheese, it's a family classic. The simple version of this recipe can be used as a vegetarian dish, but I will give a non-vegetarian alternative which I think takes it to new heights. I serve this particular version with Boiled Bacon (see p. 113) in place of the barley stew.

SERVES 4–6

50 g (2 oz) unsalted butter	Salt
3 onions, sliced	2 tablespoons olive oil (optional)
350 g (12 oz) leeks, shredded	100 g (4 oz) mature Cheddar, grated
350 g (12 oz) dried or fresh macaroni	1 teaspoon English mustard (optional)

For the Béchamel Sauce

50 g (2 oz) unsalted butter	750 ml (1¼ pints) milk
50 g (2 oz) plain flour	150 ml (5 fl oz) double cream

For the Reduction (optional)

1 carrot, chopped	1 small garlic clove, crushed
1 onion, chopped	1 sprig of fresh thyme
1 leek, chopped	300 ml (10 fl oz) dry white wine
2 celery sticks, chopped	600 ml (1 pint) Chicken Stock
25 g (1 oz) unsalted butter	(see p. 228)

To make the reduction, cook all the chopped vegetables in butter with a lid on for 10 minutes with the garlic and thyme. Add the white wine and boil until reduced by two-thirds. Add the chicken stock and continue to boil until reduced by half. Keep to one side.

To start the sauce, melt the butter in a pan, stir in the flour and cook over a low heat for 10 minutes. Warm the milk in a separate pan and slowly pour it into the flour and butter, stirring all the time. When all the warm milk has been added, cook the sauce on a low heat for about 30 minutes, stirring occasionally. If you are making the simple version, just add the cream, warm through and use as described below. However, it's at this stage that you add the reduction with all the vegetables still in it. Cook this for about 10 minutes to infuse all the flavours, add the double cream and bring to the simmer. Push the sauce through a sieve. You now have a quite runny, rich cream sauce ready for its garnish and macaroni.

To cook the garnish leeks and onions, melt the butter, add the sliced onions and cook for 2–3 minutes. Add the shredded leeks and cook on a high heat for a further 2–3 minutes, stirring frequently. Remove from the heat.

If you are using dried macaroni, just follow the cooking instructions on the packet. If you have bought fresh macaroni, simply boil a pan of water with salt and 2 tablespoons of olive oil. Drop in the macaroni and cook for 4–5 minutes until tender.

Drain the pasta and mix with the leeks and onions in a pan. Pour the hot cream sauce over and stir in. The cheese can now be added but do not allow to re-boil or this will separate the cheese. Add the mustard, if using, to lift the taste. Warm through gently then serve with the boiled bacon or spoon into a flameproof vegetable dish, cover with grated cheese and glaze under a hot grill before serving as a dish on its own.

Stuffed Tomatoes with Fried Leeks

Plum tomatoes come mostly either from Italy or the USA. When cooked, they have a better taste and texture than the ordinary salad tomato. They can be found in large supermarkets, but if you can't get them just use the others. This recipe makes an attractive vegetarian main course or a tasty starter.

SERVES 4

6 large plum or salad tomatoes
Salt and freshly ground white pepper
Freshly grated nutmeg

For the Stuffing

50 g (2 oz) unsalted butter
2 shallots, sliced
350 g (12 oz) fresh spinach, stalks
   removed

500 g (1 lb) Mashed Potatoes (see p. 142)
2 tablespoons olive oil
50 g (2 oz) Cheddar or Swiss Gruyère,
   grated

For the Leek Garnish

Vegetable oil for deep-frying
2 leeks, cut into very thin 5–7.5 cm
   (2–3 in) strips
300 ml (10 fl oz) Lemon Butter Sauce
   (see p. 243)

Remove the eyes from the tomatoes and split them in half top to bottom. Scoop out and discard the seeds and juice. Season with salt and pepper.

To make the stuffing, melt the butter in a pan and cook the sliced shallots for a few minutes. Add the spinach and cook on a high heat for a further 2–3 minutes until softened. Season with salt, pepper and nutmeg. Warm the mashed potatoes and work in the olive oil.

Pre-heat the grill to hot. Place the tomatoes under the hot grill for 30 seconds to 1 minute. Remove from the heat. Spoon the spinach mixture into the tomatoes and top with the mashed potatoes (the potatoes can be piped in through a piping bag and plain nozzle). Sprinkle them with grated Cheddar or Gruyère and place under the grill until golden brown.

Meanwhile, to prepare the leek garnish, make sure the leek strips are thoroughly dry then deep-fry them in hot oil for about 30 seconds until they have crisped and taken a slight golden colour. Remove from the fat, drain well on kitchen paper and season with salt.

When the tomatoes are ready, divide them between individual bowls or plates and spoon the leeks on top. Sprinkle with a little extra olive oil or serve with the lemon butter sauce.

Bubble and Squeak

Bubble and squeak is a strange name for a vegetable dish, but I believe it's so called because of the noises the vegetables make while being fried in the pan!

As you can see in the recipe, I have given one or two alternatives. This is because bubble and squeak can really be your own invention, and either mashed or cooked potatoes, sprouts or cabbage will do the trick. I prefer mashed potatoes as this gives me more of a cake consistency, but if you're using plain boiled potatoes just peel them and cut into thick slices. The dish is usually made from left-overs so the sprouts or cabbage should be boiled or cooked. The sprouts can be sliced.

There are so many variations to a bubble and squeak. Half cabbage and half sprouts can be used, and any additions can be made: garlic, smoked bacon, leeks, herbs and so on. But as I've always said, 'Get the basics right first, then move on!'

SERVES 6–8

2 large onions, sliced
50 g (2 oz) unsalted butter
900 g (2 lb) potatoes, cooked or 750 g
    (1½ lb) left-over Mashed Potatoes
    (see p. 142)

450 g (1 lb) Brussels sprouts or green
    cabbage, cooked
Salt and freshly ground white pepper
50 g (2 oz) vegetable oil or
    dripping

Cook the sliced onions in half the butter until softened. Mix in the potatoes and sprouts or cabbage and season with salt and pepper. Pre-heat a small frying-pan and add the remaining butter and the oil or dripping. Fry the bubble mix for 6–8 minutes, pushing it down with a spatula to create a potato and vegetable cake. The pan should be kept hot, as this will create a crispy base. To turn over the bubble, cover the pan with a plate, invert the pan so the cake falls on to the plate, then slip it, uncooked side down, back into the pan and repeat the cooking process. The bubble and squeak is now ready and can be cut into six or eight wedges before serving or left whole as a cake.

OVERLEAF
Tomatoes to use in soups,
salads and so many
other dishes.

Spinach Dumplings

These make a lovely vegetarian main course or a delicious starter. I also use them as a garnish for stews and soups. They can be served in many combinations: with a spicy Tomato or Red Pepper Coulis (see p. 240), fresh herb butter or just plain melted butter – delicious!

SERVES 4

1 onion, finely chopped
100 g (4 oz) unsalted butter
550 g (1¼ lb) fresh spinach, stalks
    removed
Salt and freshly ground white pepper
225 g (8 oz) Mascarpone or full-fat soft
    cheese

225 g (8 oz) plain flour
2 eggs
1 egg yolk
A pinch of freshly grated
    nutmeg
100 g (4 oz) Parmesan,
    grated

Sweat the chopped onion in the butter for a few minutes until translucent, then allow to cool. Wash the spinach well to remove any grit, then shake off any excess water. Blanch the spinach in boiling salted water for about 30 seconds then refresh in iced water. Squeeze the spinach until all the liquid is removed then chop it finely. Mix together the spinach and onion, then fold in the soft cheese and flour. Lightly beat the eggs and egg yolk together, then add them to the mixture and season with salt, pepper and nutmeg. Leave the mixture to rest for about 15 minutes, then mould it into dumplings using floured hands, allowing three to four per portion.

The dumplings can now be cooked in simmering salted water for 10–15 minutes. While they are cooking, pre-heat the grill. Arrange the dumplings in a flameproof dish and cover with the grated Parmesan. Finish under the hot grill until the cheese is lightly browned.

*Spinach Dumplings
with Tomato Coulis
(see p. 240).*

Spinach with Shallots, Garlic and Croûtons

Any spinach dish should always be cooked just two or three minutes before you are going to eat. This way you get the maximum taste and texture. In this recipe there are one or two things that can be done in advance – the trimming and washing of the spinach, making the croûtons, and the pre-cooking of the shallots and garlic.

SERVES 4

450 g (1 lb) fresh spinach, stalks removed	2 shallots, sliced
2 slices crusty bread	1 small garlic clove, crushed
Olive oil	25 g (1 oz) unsalted butter
Salt and freshly ground white pepper	Freshly grated nutmeg

Make sure that all the central, tough stalks have been removed from the spinach leaves, and that it has been washed in cold water at least once to remove any grit. Drain well.

Dice the crusty bread into 5 mm–1 cm (¼–½ in) squares. Fry in about 5 mm (¼ in) of olive oil in a hot frying-pan or roast in the oven until golden brown. Drain well on kitchen paper then sprinkle with salt.

In a large pan, cook the sliced shallots and garlic in 1 tablespoon of olive oil and the butter for a few minutes until soft. These can now be left in the pan ready to cook the spinach.

When ready to cook the spinach, re-heat the shallots and garlic until bubbling. Add the spinach and keep on a high heat, turning the spinach in the pan. The leaves will quickly soften and after 2–3 minutes will be cooked. Season with salt, pepper and nutmeg. The crispy croûtons can now be added or just sprinkled over in the serving dish.

Spinach with Cream and Garlic

This is a good vegetable dish to accompany a number of main courses, but it goes especially well with stews and braised dishes.

SERVES 4

450 g (1 lb) fresh spinach, stalks
    removed
50 g (2 oz) unsalted butter
1 onion, finely chopped
1 garlic clove, crushed
75 ml (3 fl oz) double cream
Salt and freshly ground white pepper
Freshly grated nutmeg

Make sure you have removed all the tough stalks from the spinach and washed the leaves at least once to remove any grit. Drain off any excess water and place in a hot pan with half the butter. Cook for 1–2 minutes on a high heat then remove from the heat and leave to cool. Cut the spinach three or four times to break it down.

In a separate pan, cook the chopped onions and garlic in the remaining butter for a few minutes until soft but not coloured. Add the cream and bring to the boil. Add the spinach and cook for 2 minutes. Season with salt, pepper and nutmeg and serve at once.

Braised Split Peas

The classic dishes of Boiled Bacon (see p. 113) and battered deep-fried cod go very well with these braised peas. I also like to make Split Pea Fritters and serve them with Home-made Pork Sausages (see p. 116).

SERVES 6–8

100 g (4 oz) carrots
2 celery sticks
2 onions
1 garlic clove, chopped
1 tablespoon olive oil
25 g (1 oz) unsalted butter
450 g (1 lb) dried split peas
About 900 ml (1½ pints) Vegetable
    Stock (see p. 229) or Chicken Stock
    (see p. 228)
Salt and freshly ground white pepper

Pre-heat the oven to 200°C/400°F/gas 6.

Cut the carrots, celery and onions into 5 mm (¼ in) dice. Sweat with the garlic in the olive oil and butter for a few minutes in a flameproof casserole dish. Add the split peas and cook for 1–2 minutes, stirring. Cover with the stock and bring to the simmer. Cover and cook in the pre-heated oven for 20–25 minutes. The peas will need stirring during cooking, and possibly more stock will need to be added. After 30 minutes the peas should be ready, just starting to break and tender to eat. Season with salt and pepper before serving.

Buttered Spetzli with Leeks

What are spetzli? Well, really, they're just simple little dumplings. They can be served with stews and casseroles, or just as a vegetable dish, and they go particularly well with the marinated lamb chumps on p. 133.

SERVES 4

350 g (12 oz) plain flour
4 eggs
1 egg yolk
2 tablespoons double cream or milk
Salt and freshly ground white pepper
Freshly grated nutmeg

To serve

50 g (2 oz) unsalted butter
1 tablespoon olive oil
225 g (8 oz) leeks, finely shredded
(optional)

Place the flour in a bowl and make a well in the centre. Add all the other spetzli ingredients and carefully mix in. When all is mixed together, beat with a wooden spoon to make the mixture a little lighter. It is ready when it comes away from the sides of the bowl.

To cook, fill a pan with salted water and bring to the boil. The spetzli can now be scraped into the water from a chopping board in small walnut-sized pieces. When these rise to the top, remove with a slotted spoon and refresh in cold water. It is best to cook them in batches of about ten or twelve.

To serve, drain the spetzli and dry them off. Melt the butter with the olive oil and fry the shredded leeks, if using, for a couple of minutes. Add the spetzli and warm through for a few minutes, then season with salt and pepper.

Braised Chicory

This can be used as a vegetable dish, or as part of a fish dish, particularly good with Mashed Potatoes (see p. 142) and Grilled Sea Bass (see p. 76).

(see p. 142) *(see p. 76)*

SERVES 4

6 heads Belgian chicory
25 g (1 oz) unsalted butter
3 tablespoons olive oil
2 shallots, sliced
1 sprig of fresh thyme
A few fresh basil leaves
A few white peppercorns
150 ml (5 fl oz) sweet white wine
600 ml (1 pint) Vegetable Stock (see
    p. 229) or Chicken Stock (see p. 228)

Split the chicory down the centre, giving you twelve pieces, three per portion. Pre-heat a frying-pan and add the butter. Fry the chicory in the butter for about 3–4 minutes until they have coloured on all sides.

In a separate pan, warm the olive oil, add the sliced shallots, herbs and peppercorns and cook for a few minutes. Add the white wine and boil to reduce until almost dry. Add the stock and boil to reduce by one-third. Sit the chicory in the stock, bring to the simmer and cook for 15–20 minutes until the chicory is tender.

Remove the chicory from the cooking liquor and keep it warm. Taste the liquor; it may well need reducing a little more to increase in strength. When ready, push the liquor through a sieve and pour over the chicory. The dish is now ready.

Wild Mushroom Risotto

Risotto is one of the most popular dishes in all of Italy. I find it exciting because it can take on so many combinations.

There are many different types of rice – from basmati to long-grain, wild and others – but for risotto the best rice to use is arborio, which can be obtained from most supermarkets and delicatessens. Arborio is a region in Italy where this rice is produced and, of course, there are several varieties available; you will find that they all make good risotto. The best is a medium-grain which has an outer layer that disintegrates during cooking, producing the starch to give a good, creamy texture.

I've used wild mushrooms in the recipe but if you find these hard to get, then just substitute with more sliced button mushrooms. The dish will still be good to eat as a starter or a vegetarian main course (see p. 159).

SERVES 4–6

1.2 litres (2 pints) Chicken or Vegetable
  Stock (see pp. 228 or 229)
100 g (4 oz) unsalted butter
2 onions, finely chopped
1 garlic clove, crushed
100 g (4 oz) button mushrooms, sliced
100 g (4 oz) fresh oyster mushrooms
  (optional)

50 g (2 oz) mixed wild mushrooms
  (optional)
50–75 g (2–3 oz) bone marrow, chopped
  (optional)
225 g (8 oz) arborio rice
50 g (2 oz) Parmesan cheese
Salt and freshly ground white pepper

Firstly heat the chicken or vegetable stock and keep it warm. Melt the butter in a large pan and add the chopped onions and garlic. Allow this to cook for 2–3 minutes without colouring. Add all the mushrooms and continue to cook and stir for a further 2–3 minutes. If this is not to be a vegetarian risotto, add the chopped bone marrow for extra richness and taste. Next, add the rice and stir continually over a low heat for a few minutes, just softening the rice.

Over a medium heat, begin to add the hot stock, a ladle at a time, allowing the rice to absorb all the stock before adding any more. Just continue to add stock gradually and stir until the rice has softened, which should take about 15–20 minutes.

Grate three-quarters of the Parmesan and slice the remainder as thinly as possible into flakes, or use a potato peeler. When the rice is ready, season with salt and pepper and stir in the grated Parmesan. The finished dish should be light and creamy. Sprinkle with the remaining Parmesan flakes, and serve.

" Lots of stirring and lots of steam – the secret of a good risotto. "

Wild Mushroom Risotto
(see p. 157).

Fried Cabbage, Celeriac, Carrots and Bacon

This dish eats very well as a vegetable, or is delicious with Confit of Duck (see p. 98). I prefer to cook it in rich duck fat for extra taste. If you find that's not available, use olive oil. The vegetables and bacon are cooked individually in the fat then combined to give four different tastes and textures which all go very well together.

SERVES 4

50 g (2 oz) duck fat or 3 tablespoons
    olive oil
225 g (8 oz) carrots, cut into thin strips
225 g (8 oz) celeriac, cut into 1 cm
    (½ in) dice
1 garlic clove, crushed
225 g (8 oz) smoked streaky bacon
    rashers, rinded and cut into 2.5 cm
    (1 in) pieces
225 g (8 oz) Savoy cabbage leaves, cut
    into 2.5 cm (1 in) squares
Salt and freshly ground black pepper

Pre-heat a frying-pan and add some of the fat or olive oil. Fry the carrot sticks for 5–6 minutes until tender. Remove them from the pan and add a little more fat or oil. Fry the diced celeriac and garlic for a further 5 minutes and remove from the pan. Fry the bacon next; this will only take about 2 minutes in the hot pan. Lastly add the cabbage and cook for 2–3 minutes. Mix them all together and season with salt and pepper. This dish can be made in advance and then all reheated, seasoned and fried together when needed.

Glazed Carrots

Cooking carrots in this way really lifts a basic vegetable into a complete dish. They also eat very well with the Pigs' Cheeks Stew (see p. 108), whether it is made with pigs' cheeks or duck legs.

SERVES 4

750 g (1½ lb) carrots
600 ml (1 pint) Vegetable Stock (see
    p. 229)
100 g (4 oz) unsalted butter
Salt and freshly ground white pepper
½ teaspoon caster sugar (optional)

Split the carrots lengthways and then cut into 1 cm (½ in) pieces diagonally. Cover them with the vegetable stock, add the butter and bring to a simmer. Cook for 10–12 minutes. The carrots should now be ready.

Drain the cooking liquor into a separate pan and boil to reduce by three-quarters. This reduction will be quite thick and very shiny. Season with salt and pepper and add a little sugar if you think it could be sweeter. Add the carrots and simmer for 2–3 minutes, turning them in the glaze before serving.

OVERLEAF
Never overlook everyday vegetables.
A simple recipe can transform
them into a delicious dish.

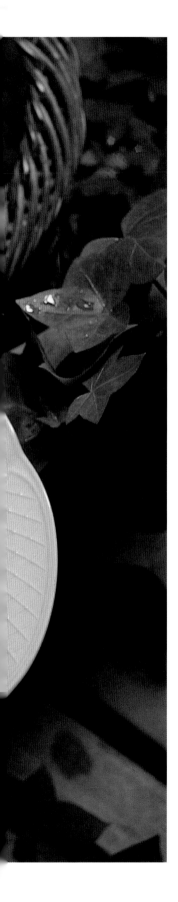

Puddings

This will be a lot of people's favourite chapter. We all love puddings, and we probably all eat far too many of them! The British are well known for their national sweet tooth, and there is a wealth of great traditional recipes for puddings, creams, fruit tarts and pies, and ices etc. It is said we liked sweet things so much that we had to invent an extra meal at which to enjoy them – afternoon tea – and so there are a few recipes here for teacakes and pastries (Gingerbread Cake, Banana and Pecan Nut Bread, Chocolate Flan and Semolina Tart among them).

ABOVE *Glazed Lemon Tart*
(see p. 202).
LEFT *Summer Pudding with cream*
(see p. 178).

167

Most of the recipes here are British in origin, with one or two exceptions. The easiest of them all is the Lemon Posset: just cream, lemon and sugar. The finished texture eats just like a mousse, so if you're looking for a quick pudding for some unexpected visitors or for a dinner party, then this is the one for you. Crumbles are very British, and are a great excuse for experimenting with any seasonal fruit. Rice puddings can be eaten hot or cold, a sherry trifle is wonderful when made well, and I love steamed sponge puddings, especially when served with a home-made custard.

A lot of the most famous British puddings are made with bread – Summer Pudding, Queen of Puddings, and one of my own favourites, Bread and Butter Pudding. Now this pudding really has seen some changes. It's usually associated with stale bread, butter, a couple of eggs, sugar and milk, and then it's baked on its own in the oven until firm – ugh! That's not what I call bread and butter pudding. I think of it as almost sponge-like in texture with thick fresh custard just oozing out between the layers. The best thing to do is just turn to page 184, follow the recipe, and then I promise you'll never look back. Here's wishing you happy puddings!

Crème Brûlée

I've never been quite sure if this originates from France or England, but I've always called it crème brûlée *(see overleaf). It sounds a lot tastier than 'burnt cream'. This recipe is very similar to the Anglaise Sauce (see p. 220) but is cooked in a slightly different way and certainly has a different finish.*

SERVES 6

8 egg yolks
50 g (2 oz) caster sugar
600 ml (1 pint) double cream

1 vanilla pod, split, or a few drops of
  good vanilla essence
Icing sugar

Pre-heat the oven to 180°C/350°F/gas 4.

Mix the egg yolks and sugar together well in a bowl. Bring the cream to the boil with the vanilla pod, if using. Remove the vanilla pod and scrape the insides into the cream. Now whisk the cream into the egg yolks and sugar. Sit the bowl over a pan of hot water and heat until the custard begins to thicken, stirring all the time. It should have the consistency of single cream. It is now ready for the next stage.

Divide the custard between six 7.5 cm (3 in) ramekins or moulds. Sit these in a roasting tin and add warm water until it comes three-quarters up the sides of the moulds. Finish in the pre-heated oven until just setting, about 20–30 minutes. To test, remove one of the moulds from the water after 20 minutes and shake gently. There should still be slight movement in the centre of the custard. If it is still runny, put it back in the oven and check after another 5 minutes. Remove from the oven and allow to cool. I prefer to eat these at room temperature, so I do not put them in the fridge.

To finish the brûlées, when set sprinkle them liberally with icing sugar. If you have a blow torch, this is great for achieving a quick and even glaze! If not, then colour them under a pre-heated hot grill, having the moulds as close as possible to the heat. As the sugar is heating, it will bubble and start to colour. More sugar may need to be added and then continue to colour until deep golden brown. The brûlée is now ready to serve.

Variation

You can make chocolate brûlées by simply adding grated chocolate to the mix before putting it into the ramekins. About 100 g (4 oz) of good-quality plain chocolate should be enough for this recipe – but of course if you prefer it stronger, just add some more! The brûlées can be finished with icing sugar, but I think they are better when topped with chocolate shavings.

Cappuccino Mousse

I always enjoy a cappuccino coffee – it's lovely with the frothy milk on top – so I thought, why not have a pudding to match? Chocolate and coffee go so well with each other, and the lightly whipped cream on top is a really good finish to the dish.

If you make your own biscuits it would be very nice to offer cappuccino mousse and biscuits for pudding. Why not try the home-made Palmier Biscuits (see p. 218)?

SERVES 4

175 g (6 oz) plain chocolate
3 tablespoons strong black coffee
5 egg whites

50 g (2 oz) caster sugar
2 egg yolks
150 ml (5 fl oz) double cream, whipped

Break 150 g (5 oz) of the chocolate into small pieces and melt with the coffee in a bowl over a pan of hot water. Beat the egg whites with the sugar to a meringue consistency, creating soft peaks. Fold the egg yolks into the melted chocolate, making sure it is not too hot, add one-third of the egg white meringue and whisk into the chocolate. Carefully fold in the remaining egg whites and half of the whipped cream.

The mousse can now be spooned into glasses, ramekin dishes or one large bowl and placed in the fridge for 2–3 hours to set. The remaining cream can be piped or forked on top of the mousse. To finish the dish, just finely grate the remaining chocolate over the top. So now we have a cappuccino coffee pudding with extra chocolate taste.

Chocolate Sponge Cake with Cappuccino Mousse

If you would like to be more adventurous, here is a way to make the mousse even more exciting. The sponge adds a good texture to the mousse, but of course can be used with any mousse or other puddings.

PREVIOUS PAGE
Finishing the Crème Brûlée: if you don't own a blow torch then a pre-heated hot grill will achieve the same deep golden brown colour (see p. 169).

SERVES 4

1 quantity Cappuccino Mousse
    (see left)
Rum or liqueur to taste
1 quantity Coffee Sauce
    (see p. 220) or Clementine or
    Orange Sauce (see p. 221)
1 sprig of fresh mint

For the Sponge

175 g (6 oz) plain chocolate
3 tablespoons strong black coffee
5 eggs, separated
100 g (4 oz) caster sugar
Pinch of salt

Pre-heat the oven to 180°C/350°F/gas 4 and line a 30 × 25 cm (12 × 10 in) baking tray and four 6 cm (2½ in) flan rings with greaseproof paper to come up 5–7 cm (2–3 in) round the sides.

To make the sponge, melt the chocolate with the coffee in a bowl over a pan of hot water. Leave to cool slightly. Beat the egg yolks until smooth then add the caster sugar. Continue to beat until pale and the mixture trails off the whisk in ribbons. In a separate bowl, beat the egg whites and salt until they form soft peaks. Add the melted chocolate to the egg yolk mix then fold in the egg whites. Spread on to the lined baking tray to between 5 mm (¼ in) and 1 cm (½ in) thick. Bake in the pre-heated oven for 15 minutes. Remove from the oven and allow to cool.

Make the mousse but do not allow it to set. Cut out four rings from the sponge the same diameter as the flan rings, and place them in the bottom of the rings. The sponge can now be flavoured with a little rum or liqueur, if required. Spoon the mousse into the moulds on top of the sponge, chill and leave to set.

When the mousses are set, lift off the flan rings and carefully take off the paper. Finish with the whipped cream and grated chocolate of the mousse recipe. Place the mousses on plates and serve with your chosen sauce and a sprig of mint.

ABOVE AND OPPOSITE
*Lemon Posset – a simple pudding
for everyone to enjoy*
(see p. 176).

66 *If you're stuck for a pudding*
And pushed for time,
Then turn to this recipe
And you'll be fine. **99**

Lemon Posset

This must be the easiest pudding to prepare and cook, which is why I've included it in the book (see previous page).

(see previous page)

SERVES 6

900 ml (1½ pints) double cream
250 g (9 oz) caster sugar
Juice of 3 lemons

Boil the cream and sugar together in a pan and cook for 2–3 minutes. Add the lemon juice and mix in well. Leave to cool slightly then pour into six glasses and leave to set in the fridge. The pudding is now ready. It is nice to pour a little more liquid cream on top before serving.

Sherry Trifle

Trifle over the years has taken on many variations. The word itself comes from an old term, 'trifling', which meant layering different sponges, fruits and jellies, and finished with a sabayon rather than a custard. Of course, most home-made trifles still have all those ingredients, even sometimes blancmange too, but as with most other things, I like good old-fashioned simplicity, and this recipe has plenty of taste and texture, without all the extras.

The custard below can be used solely for this pudding, but I like to go halves with Anglaise Sauce (see p. 220) to give a richer and fresher taste. (I don't use all Anglaise because it wouldn't set.)

SERVES 4

For the Sponge

3 eggs
75 g (3 oz) caster sugar
75 g (3 oz) plain flour
40 g (1½ oz) unsalted butter, melted

For the Syrup

225 g (8 oz) caster sugar
300 ml (10 fl oz) water
4–5 tablespoons sweet sherry

For the Custard Sauce

600 ml (1 pint) milk
50 g (2 oz) custard powder
50 g (2 oz) caster sugar

For the Filling and Topping

Raspberry jam to cover the sponge
300 ml (10 fl oz) double cream, whipped
100 g (4 oz) plain chocolate, grated

Pre-heat the oven to 200°C/400°F/gas 6 and grease and line a 20 cm (8 in) flan tin or flan ring and baking sheet.

To make the sponge, whisk the eggs and sugar in a bowl over a pan of hot water until the mixture has doubled in bulk and is light and creamy. Very gently fold in the flour and melted butter. Pour the mix into the lined flan tin or ring and bake in the pre-heated oven for 30 minutes. Turn out and allow to cool.

To make the syrup, boil the sugar and water together for about 2 minutes to a syrup, then add sherry to taste – more than above if you like the taste.

To make the custard sauce, mix some of the milk with the custard powder in a pan. Bring the remaining milk to the boil in another pan. Pour this on to the custard powder, whisking all the time. Return to the heat and bring back to the boil. While stirring, the sauce will thicken. Add the sugar, cover with buttered greaseproof paper and allow to cool.

Split the sponge in half horizontally and spread jam on both pieces. Place one half into a bowl and soak with half the sherry syrup. Sit the other sponge on top and again soak with sherry syrup. Pour the custard on top and allow to set in the fridge. When set, spoon the whipped cream on top and sprinkle with grated chocolate.

You can also make individual trifles in 10 cm (4 in) soufflé dishes. Bake little sponges to fit, or cut to fit, and assemble in exactly the same way.

Summer Pudding

I've listed quantities and varieties of fruits below but, of course, the beauty of this dish is that the choice of red berries is entirely your own, so use what is easily available (see pp. 166–7). I have found that these fruits work well together. You need about 1.4 kg (3 lb) of soft fruit altogether. If there is a lot of the fruit mix left over it can be kept for a few days and served as it is with ice-cream or cream – or make some more puddings!

Serves 8–10

2 punnets raspberries
2 punnets strawberries
1 punnet tayberries or loganberries
1 punnet blackberries
1 punnet redcurrants

1 punnet blackcurrants
1 punnet blueberries
2 tablespoons crème de
    framboises
1 loaf thinly sliced white bread

For the Raspberry Purée

450 g (1 lb) fresh or frozen raspberries
50 g (2 oz) icing sugar

For the Sugar Syrup

600 ml (1 pint) water
350 g (12 oz) caster sugar

To serve

Clotted or whipped cream

Lightly butter a 1.5 litre (2½ pint) basin or eight 150 ml (5 fl oz) moulds.

Trim and wash all the fruits and leave to drain.

To make the raspberry purée, simply blitz the berries and sugar together in a blender, then push through a sieve.

To make the sugar syrup, simply boil the water and sugar together for a few minutes to a clear syrup. Leave to cool.

Mix half of the raspberry purée with the sugar syrup and bring to the simmer. Add the fruits and the crème de framboises to the sauce, then remove from the heat and leave to rest. The fruits should have all softened but will still have kept their shape. When cool, pour some of the syrup into a separate bowl.

Remove the crusts from the bread and cut each slice into three. Dip these in the reserved raspberry syrup and line the basin or moulds with the soaked bread, overlapping slightly with each slice. When the basin or all the moulds are lined, fill with the fruits and a little of the sauce and cover with more bread. Cover with a plate, press down with a weight and leave in the fridge for a few hours.

Mix the remaining raspberry purée with a little of the remaining pudding juices until you have a sauce consistency. Turn out the summer puddings on to plates or divide the large one into wedges, and spoon the finished raspberry sauce over them. Garnish with some of the remaining fruit mix, purée and clotted or whipped cream.

OVERLEAF
*Summer fruits for
Summer Pudding.*

Vanilla Ice-cream

Many alternatives can be made from this basic vanilla ice-cream recipe, a few of which I have outlined below.

In the basic recipe, vanilla pods are used. These can be quite expensive, but if you buy two or three pods and keep them in an airtight container with caster sugar, you will have all the taste you want in the sugar for the recipe. You can, of course, use the pods again and again by just topping up the container with more sugar. Failing this, a good, thick vanilla essence will also work.

SERVES 4–6

1 vanilla pod
300 ml (10 fl oz) double cream
300 ml (10 fl oz) milk
6 egg yolks
175 g (6 oz) caster sugar

Split the vanilla pod and scrape the insides into the cream and milk in a pan. Bring to the boil.

While the milk and cream are heating, mix the egg yolks and sugar together in a bowl and beat until pale. When the cream has boiled, pour slowly on to the egg yolks and sugar, beating all the time. Continue to stir until the ice-cream mixture has cooled. Once cooled, chill until totally cold. The mix is now ready to make into ice-cream.

Pour into an ice-cream maker and turn until the cream has thickened, increased in volume and, of course, frozen. If you do not have an ice-cream maker, pour the mix into a suitable container and place in the freezer, stirring well every 30 minutes until frozen. The beating is important to get the correct, smooth texture. You should now have a thick dairy ice-cream which will be best served as soon as made or frozen for a minimum time.

Variations

This recipe can now be used for many alternatives. To make fruit ice-creams add a fruit purée. Or, the vanilla can be replaced with cinnamon sticks left in the mixture until cold, or 1–2 teaspoons of ground cinnamon. This can be served with apple fritters, apple tart, or even a good old-fashioned apple crumble (see p. 198 and 200).

Fruit Ice-cream

This is a simple recipe which uses a stock syrup (also used in sorbet-making). Crème fraîche is French 'fresh' cream, and is now available in most supermarkets. It is cream that has been treated with a special culture which gives it a longer life and an almost sour taste. It works very well in ice-creams, giving a full body to the taste.

SERVES 4–6

300 ml (10 fl oz) fruit purée (strawberry,
    raspberry, mango etc.)
1–2 heaped tablespoons crème fraîche

For the Stock Syrup

300 ml (10 fl oz) water
225 g (8 oz) caster sugar, flavoured with
    vanilla (see left)
1 tablespoon liquid glucose (optional)

To make the stock syrup, simply bring all the ingredients to the boil and cook for 2–3 minutes. This will leave you with a thick, sweet syrup. Leave until cold.

To make the fruit ice, mix the fruit purée with the cold stock syrup and add the crème fraîche. The mix is now ready to freeze, either in a machine or freezer, churning by hand every now and again.

Praline

Another lovely ice-cream is made with praline, a toffee-type mixture of sugar and hazelnuts boiled together. Simply crush the praline pieces in a bowl and add to the vanilla ice-cream mix when it's ready to be churned or frozen. This will be very sweet so it's best to omit 50 g (2 oz) of caster sugar from the basic ice-cream recipe.

100 g (4 oz) shelled hazelnuts, chopped
100 g (4 oz) caster sugar

Place the nuts and sugar together in a pan and slowly cook until the sugar is golden brown. Pour the mixture on to a lightly oiled tray and leave until set and cold. The praline is now ready to break.

Sorbets

Sorbets are also known as water ices. They are good as a light pudding or to serve between courses as a palate cleanser. All you need is to mix equal quantities of stock syrup and fruit purée, exactly as the fruit ice-creams, but without the crème fraîche.

For example, 300 ml (10 fl oz) each of stock syrup and an apple purée mixed together and turned through an ice-cream maker will produce a simple sorbet. This, of course, can be improved by adding a squeeze of lemon juice to enrich the taste and some cider or calvados to make it even stronger.

All sorbets can be made and varied in this way. A raspberry sorbet can be really tasty with a little raspberry liqueur added in place of some of the stock syrup.

These sorbets can be used as a main item for puddings. How does a pear sorbet with chocolate sauce and fresh thick cream sound?

Bread and Butter Pudding

Bread and butter pudding has become one of our great classics. It was always a good way of using up stale bread with milk, sugar and eggs, but this would often result in a firm and tasteless pud, which left it with a bad name. This recipe will give you quite a different dish (see pp. 186–7). I'm using just egg yolks and half milk and double cream, which is obviously a little more expensive to make, but once you've tried it you'll never want to make it any other way!

SERVES 6–8

12 medium slices white bread	300 ml (10 fl oz) milk
50 g (2 oz) unsalted butter, softened	300 ml (10 fl oz) double cream
8 egg yolks	25 g (1 oz) sultanas
175 g (6 oz) caster sugar	25 g (1 oz) raisins
1 vanilla pod or a few drops of vanilla essence	

To finish

Caster sugar

Grease a 1.75 litre (3 pint) pudding basin with butter.

Firstly, remove the crusts and butter the bread. Whisk the egg yolks and caster sugar together in a bowl. Split the vanilla pod and place in a pan with the milk and cream. Bring the milk and cream to the simmer, then sieve on to the egg yolks, stirring all the time. You now have the custard.

Arrange the bread in layers in the prepared basin, sprinkling the sultanas and raisins in between layers. Finish with a final layer of bread without any fruit on top as this tends to burn. The warm egg mixture may now be poured over the bread and cooked straightaway, but I prefer to pour the custard over the pudding then leave it to soak into the bread for 20 minutes before cooking. This allows the bread to take on a new texture and have the flavours all the way through.

Pre-heat the oven to 180°C/350°F/gas 4.

Once the bread has been soaked, place the dish in a roasting tray three-quarters filled with warm water and place in the pre-heated oven. Cook for about 20–30 minutes in the pre-heated oven until the pudding begins to set. Because we are using only egg yolks, the mixture cooks like a fresh custard and only thickens; it should not become too firm.

When ready, remove from the water bath, sprinkle liberally with caster sugar to cover, and glaze under the grill on medium heat. The sugar should dissolve and caramelize and you may find that the corners of the bread start to burn a little. This helps the flavours, though, giving a bittersweet taste, and certainly looks good. The bread and butter pudding is now ready to serve and when you take that first spoonful and place it into a bowl you will see the custard just seeping from the dish – it's delicious!

Bread and Butter Pudding
(see p. 184).

Glazed Pear and Almond Zabaglione

This dish looks very simple and almost like a crème brûlée, but just think of all those textures and tastes. When you break through the sugar topping it's into the warm zabaglione then on to the cooked pears and finally the moist almond sponge. I've chosen Comice pears because they have a good, sweet taste and texture. Other varieties will work but may need more cooking and more sugar to taste. This dish comes in a very close second to the bread and butter pudding!

The frangipane or almond sponge recipe is wonderful for home-made bakewell tart, bakewell and apple tart, or prune, Armagnac and almond tart. Because of the high ratio of ground almonds, it's very moist and keeps a lot longer than a traditional sponge.

SERVES 4–6

6 Comice pears
50 g (2 oz) icing sugar
1 tablespoon unsalted butter

For the Almond Sponge (Frangipane)

225 g (8 oz) unsalted butter
225 g (8 oz) caster sugar
50 g (2 oz) plain flour
175 g (6 oz) ground almonds
4 eggs

For the Zabaglione

5 egg yolks
40 g (1½ oz) caster sugar
25 ml (1 fl oz) Poire Williams (Marsala
    or Calvados will both work)
25 ml (1 fl oz) dry white wine

Pre-heat the oven to 200°C/400°F/gas 6 and grease and line a 20 cm (8 in) square baking tray.

To make the sponge, beat the butter and sugar until creamed. Add the flour and ground almonds and stir until well blended. Add one egg at a time, making sure it is completely beaten in before adding the next. This process can be done in a food processor or mixer, or with a plain wooden spoon. When everything is thoroughly folded in, spread the mix 1 cm (½ in) thick in the prepared baking tray. Bake in the pre-heated oven for 20–30 minutes until firm and set. Allow to cool.

Meanwhile, prepare the pears. Peel and chop two of the pears and cook quickly in a pan with a tablespoon of icing sugar and the butter. These pears need to cook to a purée. When very soft, push them through a sieve. Peel and cut the remaining pears into 1 cm (½ in) dice. Bring the purée to the boil and add the diced pears. Cook for just 2–3 minutes on a high heat then allow to cool slightly.

Cut the sponge into rounds to fit four 9 cm (3½ in) soufflé moulds or one 23 cm (9 in) bowl. Spoon the warm pears on top of the sponge.

To make the zabaglione, beat together the egg yolks and sugar until light in colour. Add the Poire Williams and white wine and whisk in a bowl over a pan of hot water until light, thick and frothy. This will take 5–10 minutes. The zabaglione should be thick enough to make soft peaks when the whisk is drawn from the mix. Spoon over the pears in the moulds or bowl.

Sieve the remaining icing sugar on top of each mould or on to the bowl. Place under a hot grill for a few minutes until golden brown. If you are very generous with the icing sugar, it will also give a crunchy topping.

Caramel Rice Pudding

This recipe shows how a simple pudding can become a great dessert!

SERVES 6

For the Caramel

225 g (8 oz) caster sugar
300 ml (10 fl oz) water

For the Pudding

225 g (8 oz) short-grain rice
1.2 litres (2 pints) milk
100 g (4 oz) caster sugar
50 g (2 oz) unsalted butter
8 egg yolks
300 ml (10 fl oz) double cream

Pre-heat the oven to 180°C/350°F/gas 4.

Prepare the caramel for the moulds first. Dissolve the sugar in three-quarters of the water, bring to the boil then boil for a few minutes without shaking the pan until the caramel is golden brown. Add the remaining water and re-boil. The caramel is now ready and can be divided between six 9 cm (3½ in) soufflé dishes. Leave to set.

To make the pudding, place the rice in cold water to cover, bring to the boil, then drain, refresh under cold water and drain again. Boil 1 litre (1¾ pints) of the milk, half the sugar and the butter in a large pan and add the rice. Bring to the simmer and cook for about 8–10 minutes until tender. Beat the egg yolks and remaining sugar together in a bowl. Boil the cream with the remaining milk. Pour the milk on to the yolks, stirring all the time. Mix this with the rice, then pour carefully into the caramel-lined moulds. Stand the moulds in a baking tray three-quarters filled with hot water and bake in the pre-heated oven for about 20–30 minutes until set. When set, remove from the water bath and leave to cool.

The puddings must now be chilled until firm and totally set. Release from the dishes with a warm knife and turn out. The rice puddings will hold together with the custard, and the caramel will pour over the top.

Rhubarb Rice Pudding

This is a delicious pudding which combines a traditional rice pudding with the slightly sharp taste of the rhubarb.

SERVES 6

450 g (1 lb) rhubarb
25 g (1 oz) unsalted butter
100 g (4 oz) caster sugar
1 quantity Rice Pudding mixture
 (see left)
75 g (3 oz) icing sugar

Pre-heat the oven to 180°C/350°F/gas 4.

Lightly peel the rhubarb and cut into 2.5 cm (1 in) pieces. Melt the butter in a pan and cook the rhubarb and caster sugar over a high heat for about 4–5 minutes until soft, stirring frequently. This should now be tasted to see if it is sweet enough. Allow the rhubarb to drain through a sieve, keeping any syrup. Spoon the rhubarb into six 9 cm (3½ in) soufflé dishes, only filling them about one-third deep.

Make the rice pudding mix as described in the previous recipe, then add the reserved syrup to the rice pudding mixture and use this to cover the rhubarb. Stand the moulds in a baking tray three-quarters filled with hot water and bake in the pre-heated oven for about 20–30 minutes until set.

Remove the moulds from the water bath, sprinkle liberally with the icing sugar and glaze under a hot grill. Unlike the caramel rice pudding, this can be served hot and left in the moulds.

Manchester Pudding
(Queen of Puddings)

This is a really sweet pudding, the one you want to eat plenty of but always regret afterwards! Here are two recipes which both work very well. The one using breadcrumbs is the more traditional, but the sponge and jam one is also delicious. The beauty of using sponge is that you can use up your Madeira cake when it's past its best.

SERVES 4–6

RECIPE 1

600 ml (1 pint) milk
Zest of 1 lemon
50 g (2 oz) unsalted butter
50 g (2 oz) caster sugar

100 g (4 oz) fresh white breadcrumbs
6 egg yolks
4 tablespoons raspberry jam

For the Meringue

4 egg whites
225 g (8 oz) caster sugar

Pre-heat the oven to 180°C/350°F/gas 4 and prepare six 7.5 cm (3 in) soufflé dishes or one 1.75 litre (3 pint) soufflé dish.

Bring the milk and lemon rind to the boil in a pan, then remove from the heat and leave to stand for 15 minutes. Remove the zest and add the butter and sugar. Bring back to the simmer and remove from the heat. Stir in the breadcrumbs and allow to cool slightly. Beat the egg yolks and add to the mix. Pour it into the soufflé dish or dishes and stand them in a roasting tray filled three-quarters full of hot water. Bake in the pre-heated oven for 30–40 minutes until set. When the puddings have just set, remove from the oven and the water bath and leave to rest for 10 minutes.

Increase the oven temperature to 230°C/450°F/gas 8. Divide the jam between the tops of the puddings. To make the meringue, whisk the egg whites with the sugar until they form firm peaks. Pipe or spoon the meringue over the top of the puddings and return them to the hot oven, or place under a pre-heated grill, for about 6–8 minutes until golden brown. The queen of puddings is now ready to serve.

RECIPE 2

½ baked Vanilla Sponge (see p. 214)
Raspberry jam
4 eggs
75 g (3 oz) caster sugar

300 ml (10 fl oz) milk
300 ml (10 fl oz) double cream
1 vanilla pod, split (optional)

For the Meringue

4 egg whites
225 g (8 oz) caster sugar

Pre-heat the oven to 160°C/325°F/gas 3 and prepare six 7.5 cm (3 in) soufflé dishes or one 1.75 litre (3 pint) soufflé dish.

Split the sponge into three layers and sandwich together again with the raspberry jam. Cut into 1 cm (½ in) squares and divide between the soufflé dishes or arrange in the base of the large dish.

Whisk the eggs and sugar together and add the milk, cream and the scraped out insides of the vanilla pod, if using. Strain through a sieve and pour on top of the sponge sandwich. Sit the moulds in a roasting tray three-quarters filled with hot water and cook in the pre-heated oven for 30–40 minutes until the custard has just set. Remove from the oven and the water bath and leave to rest.

Increase the oven temperature to 230°C/450°F/gas 8.

To make the meringues, whisk the egg whites with the sugar until they form firm peaks. Pipe or spoon the meringue over the top of the puddings and return them to the hot oven for about 6–8 minutes until golden brown.

So here are two ways, now you can decide which one to try!

Toffee and Banana Crumble

We've all had apple, rhubarb or apricot crumbles, but this one is almost a banana and toffee pie, which makes it a crumble with a difference!

SERVES 4

1 × 200 g (7 oz) tin condensed milk
225 g (8 oz) Puff Pastry (see p. 216)
225 g (8 oz) plain flour
100 g (4 oz) unsalted butter
100 g (4 oz) caster sugar
3 bananas

To make the toffee, place the unopened tin of condensed milk in a pan of water and boil for 3 hours, topping up with boiling water as necessary. Leave the tin to cool, and the toffee is ready!

Pre-heat the oven to 180°C/350°F/gas 4 and dampen a 25 cm (10 in) flan tin or individual flan rings on a baking sheet.

While the tin is boiling, roll out the pastry and use to line the flan tin or rings. Line the pastry with greaseproof paper, fill with baking beans and bake blind in the pre-heated oven for 15 minutes. Remove the beans and paper and leave to cool. Increase the oven temperature to 220°C/425°F/gas 7.

To make the crumble, rub the flour and butter together until the mix is like fine crumbs, then add the sugar. Chop the bananas and spoon into the flan cases. Top with the toffee from the tin and sprinkle with the crumble. Bake in the pre-heated oven for about 15–20 minutes until the crumble is golden brown. The pudding is ready to serve, and will eat very well with fresh cream or custard, or even both!

OPPOSITE
Toffee and Banana Crumble
with Anglaise Sauce (see p. 220) and cream.

Steamed Victoria Plum Pudding

A lemon sponge was the first of my steamed puddings, and I still think it can never be repeated. But here's one that comes very close! It is best served with a warm Anglaise Sauce (see p. 220).

SERVES 6

225 g (8 oz) caster sugar
300 ml (10 fl oz) water
750 g (1½ lb) Victoria plums, stoned
    and chopped

For the Sponge

100 g (4 oz) unsalted butter
150 g (5 oz) caster sugar
1 vanilla pod, split
2 eggs
1 egg yolk
200 g (7 oz) self-raising flour
Finely grated zest and juice of ½ lemon

Grease six 150 ml (5 fl oz) moulds or one 900 ml (1½ pint) basin with butter.

Dissolve the sugar in the water then bring to the boil and boil for a few minutes to make a syrup. Add the plums and cook gently for about 8–10 minutes to a lumpy, marmalade consistency.

To make the sponge, mix the butter and sugar together until almost white, then add the insides of the vanilla pod and beat in the eggs and egg yolk. Fold in the flour, lemon juice and zest. Spoon some of the plums and their syrup into the bottom of the moulds or basin. Cover with the sponge mix to come three-quarters up the sides. Cover with buttered foil and place in a steamer or a pan half-full of hot water. The small puddings will only need 40 minutes in the hot steamer, the large pudding will need 1–1½ hours.

When cooked, turn the puddings out on to a plate or plates and spoon some more of the hot Victoria plum syrup over each portion. The dish is now ready to serve and will eat well with either fresh cream or Anglaise Sauce (see p. 220).

Walnut and Maple Syrup Sponge

Sweet suet sponges have a thicker and denser texture, so I always think they need stronger tastes. The syrup helps the taste, the walnuts help the texture.

SERVES 6

175 g (6 oz) self-raising flour
75 g (3 oz) dried suet
75 g (3 oz) caster sugar
1 egg
1 egg yolk
About 2 tablespoons milk
175 g (6 oz) shelled walnuts, chopped
8 tablespoons maple syrup

Grease a 900 ml (1½ pint) or six 150 ml (5 fl oz) pudding basin(s) with butter.

Mix the flour, suet and sugar together. Beat the egg with the egg yolk then mix it into the dry ingredients. Add a little milk to give the mixture a pudding consistency when the mix just drops from the spoon. Add half the walnuts and half the maple syrup. Pour into the prepared pudding basin, cover and cook in a hot steamer or a pan half-filled with hot water for 1¼–1½ hours.

Warm the remaining walnuts in the maple syrup. Turn out the puddings on to one large or several individual plates, spoon the syrup and nuts over and serve with cream or custard.

Apple Fritters with Apricot Sauce and Vanilla Ice-cream

If it's a hot pudding you're after, this must be one of the easiest. So many other fruits can be used – bananas, apricots, pears – but I find apples go so well with the ice-cream and apricot sauce.

Serves 4

1 quantity Vanilla Ice-cream (see p. 182)

For the Apricot Sauce

225 g (8 oz) caster sugar
300 ml (10 fl oz) water
350 g (12 oz) fresh apricots, stoned and
    quartered
2 tablespoons apricot jam (optional)

For the Fritters

300 ml (10 fl oz) sweet cider
100 g (4 oz) plain flour plus a little extra
    for coating
25 g (1 oz) caster sugar
4 Granny Smith apples, peeled
    and cored
Vegetable oil for deep-frying
1 sprig of fresh mint (optional)

To make the apricot sauce, dissolve the sugar in the water over a low heat then bring to the boil and boil for a few minutes to make a syrup. Cook the apricots in the syrup and jam for about 10 minutes until they have puréed. Push through a sieve and keep warm.

To make the fritter batter, mix the cider, flour and sugar together. Cut each of the apples into five wedges and lightly flour each piece. Dip them in the batter and deep-fry in hot oil for about 5 minutes until golden and crispy. Drain well.

To serve, lay the fritters on a plate and pour the apricot sauce next to them. Serve a large spoonful of vanilla ice-cream with each portion. For extra colour, decorate with a sprig of mint.

*Apple Fritters
with Apricot Sauce and
Vanilla Ice-cream.*

Apple Tart with its own Sorbet

This recipe gives you a tart that is hot, thin and crisp, and if you can't imagine the sorbet melting all over it you're just going to have to try it! For a variation, try flavouring the sorbet with calvados or replacing the water with cider.

SERVES 4

For the Tart

225 g (8 oz) Puff Pastry (see p. 216) or
   bought
50 g (2 oz) unsalted butter
8 Granny Smith apples

4 teaspoons caster sugar
4 tablespoons apricot jam
2 tablespoons water

For the Sorbet

225 g (8 oz) caster sugar
300 ml (10 fl oz) water

10 Granny Smith apples, peeled, cored
   and chopped

Grease one large or two smaller oven trays.

To make the tart bases, roll out the puff pastry as thinly as possible and leave to rest in the fridge. Cut the pastry into four 20 cm (8 in) circles, each forming one portion. Lay the tart bases on to the oven trays and return to the fridge.

The next step is to make the sorbet. Dissolve the sugar in the water over a low heat then bring to the boil and boil for a few minutes to make a syrup. Add the apples and simmer gently for about 10–15 minutes until they start to purée. When ready, push them through a sieve and wait for the mix to cool. This can now be made into a sorbet by freezing in an ice-cream maker or in the freezer, when you'll have to whisk it every 15–20 minutes until frozen.

Pre-heat the oven to 230°C/450°F/gas 8.

To make the tarts, peel, core and quarter the apples. Slice the apple quarters into three or four pieces, and start to overlap them on the pastry discs all the way round until each circle of pastry is totally covered. Chop the butter and divide between the tarts. Sprinkle each one with caster sugar and bake in the pre-heated oven for about 15 minutes until the pastry is crisp and the apples have started to colour.

Boil the apricot jam with the water and brush on to the tarts to give a glazed finish. The apple tarts are now ready to serve. The sorbet may be shaped between two spoons to make a quenelle shape or simply served separately in a bowl.

Sticky Toffee Pudding

This is a good old English pudding which is made all over the country. I think this recipe originated with Francis Coulson of Sharrow Bay in Ullswater, and it works better than any of the other recipes I have tried. The best dates to use are Medjool, which come from India; they are plump and meaty, with almost a treacle taste.

SERVES 4

175 g (6 oz) dates, stoned and chopped
300 ml (10 fl oz) water
1 teaspoon bicarbonate of soda
50 g (2 oz) unsalted butter
175 g (6 oz) caster sugar
2 eggs, beaten
175 g (6 oz) self-raising flour
1 teaspoon vanilla essence

For the Sauce

300 ml (10 fl oz) double cream
50 g (2 oz) demerara sugar
2 teaspoons black treacle

Pre-heat the oven to 180°C/350°F/gas 4 and grease a 28 × 18 cm (11 × 7 in) baking tin.

Boil the dates in the water for about 5 minutes until soft, then add the bicarbonate of soda. Cream the butter and sugar together until light and fluffy, then add the eggs and beat well. Mix in the dates, flour and vanilla essence then pour into the greased baking tin and cook in the pre-heated oven for about 30–40 minutes until just firm to the touch.

To make the sauce, simply place all the ingredients in a pan over a low heat and stir together until blended, then bring to the boil. Some of this can be poured over the sponge and finished under the grill, or it can be kept totally separate and ladled over the sponge when portioned. Good, fresh, thick cream is just right for this pudding.

Glazed Lemon Tart

This tart has become a classic amongst chefs. It eats very well on its own, but I also like to eat it with warm cherries. These can be made by stoning 450 g (1 lb) of fresh cherries and cooking them in 50 g (2 oz) of unsalted butter and 50 g (2 oz) caster sugar for about 6–8 minutes. You can also add a measure of Kirsch to help the flavour. The cherries will have created their own syrup in the pan. Now simply spoon them on to the plate with a wedge of tart and serve with cream (see p. 167).

SERVES 8

1 quantity Sweet Pastry (see p. 219)
Finely grated rind of 1 lemon

For the Filling and Topping

8 egg yolks
350 g (12 oz) caster sugar
300 ml (10 fl oz) double cream
4 lemons, juice from all, finely grated
    zest from 2
Icing sugar

Make the pastry for the flan case, adding the grated lemon rind to the flour and icing sugar. Chill for 20–30 minutes.

Pre-heat the oven to 180°C/350°F/gas 4 and grease a 24 cm (9½ in) flan tin or flan ring on a baking sheet. (A 20 cm (8 in) ring will also work.)

Roll out the pastry and use to line the flan tin or ring. Line the pastry with grease-proof paper, fill with baking beans and bake blind in the pre-heated oven for 15–20 minutes. Remove the beans and paper and leave to cool. Reduce the oven temperature to 150°C/300°F/gas 2.

To make the filling, mix the egg yolks and caster sugar together until smooth, then pour on the cream and mix in the lemon juice and zest. Pour into the cooked flan case and bake in the pre-heated oven for 30–40 minutes until the tart is just set. Remove from the oven and allow to cool.

The tart is now ready to serve, but it's nice to finish it with a golden glaze. To do this, simply sprinkle each portion with icing sugar and colour briefly under a hot grill.

Chocolate Flan

Chocolate puddings can be so heavy and over-rich, but this flan has a light filling with a crisp base, packed with chocolate taste. This flan has a wonderful mousse-like texture which eats at its best with pouring cream.

SERVES 4–6

225 g (8 oz) Sweet Pastry (see p. 219)

For the Filling

3 eggs
1 egg yolk
100 g (4 oz) caster sugar
350 g (12 oz) plain chocolate
50 g (2 oz) unsalted butter
25 ml (1 fl oz) double cream
50 ml (2 fl oz) dark rum

Pre-heat the oven to 180°C/350°F/gas 4 and grease a 24 cm (9½ in) flan tin or flan ring on a baking sheet.

Make the pastry and allow to rest for 1 hour before using.

Roll out the pastry and use to line the flan tin or ring. Line the pastry with greaseproof paper, fill with baking beans and bake blind in the pre-heated oven for 20 minutes. Remove the beans and paper and leave to cool.

To make the filling, whisk the eggs, egg yolk and sugar together until light and doubled in volume. Melt the chocolate, butter, cream and rum together in a bowl over a pan of hot water. Carefully fold into the eggs until well blended. Pour this into the cooked pastry case and bake in the pre-heated oven for about 15 minutes until set. Leave the flan to cool and rest before taking off the flan ring. The flan is now ready to serve.

Semolina Tart

We've all eaten semolina pudding with jam, which probably often tasted like glue. This semolina recipe is very different and finishes with a texture similar to a baked cheesecake, with a slightly different taste.

SERVES 4

225 g (8 oz) Sweet Pastry (see p. 219)

For the Filling

1.2 litres (2 pints) milk	50 g (2 oz) semolina
100 ml (3½ fl oz) double cream	Grated zest and juice of 1 lemon
200 g (7 oz) caster sugar	A pinch of salt
50 g (2 oz) unsalted butter	100 g (4 oz) sultanas soaked in 50 ml
175 g (6 oz) polenta	(2 fl oz) dark rum

Pre-heat the oven to 180°C/350°F/gas 4 and grease a 20 cm (8 in) flan tin or flan ring on a baking sheet.

Roll out the pastry and use to line the flan tin or ring. Line the pastry with greaseproof paper, fill with baking beans and bake blind in the pre-heated oven for 20 minutes. Remove the beans and paper, trim round the top of the ring and leave to cool.

To make the filling, mix the milk, cream, sugar and butter in a pan and bring to the boil. Gradually whisk in the polenta and semolina, lemon zest and juice and salt, being careful to avoid any lumps. Transfer to a bowl and sit the bowl over a pan of hot water. Cook the mix for 20 minutes, stirring frequently, until the mix is very thick. Stir in the sultanas and rum. If the mix is too thick and slightly stodgy then simply thin down with a little more milk or cream. Pour the mix into the flan case, cover with buttered greaseproof paper to prevent a skin forming and leave to cool. The flan should not be turned out until completely set.

This eats very well on its own or with cream. As an alternative, some apple wedges cooked in butter and sugar can be placed on top, sprinkled with icing sugar and glazed under a hot grill.

Pecan Pie

Probably the most popular of all American classic dishes, this is just like a nutty treacle tart – lovely tastes with a lovely texture (see p. 207).

SERVES 4

225 g (8 oz) Sweet Pastry (see p. 219)

For the Filling

4 eggs
175 g (6 oz) caster sugar
300 ml (10 fl oz) golden syrup
A pinch of salt
A few drops of vanilla essence
225 g (8 oz) pecan nuts

Pre-heat the oven to 180°C/350°F/gas 4 and grease a 20 cm (8 in) flan tin or flan ring on a baking sheet.

Roll out the pastry and use to line the flan tin or ring. Line the pastry with greaseproof paper, fill with baking beans and bake blind in the pre-heated oven for 15–20 minutes. Remove the beans and paper and leave to cool. Increase the oven temperature to 200°C/400°F/gas 6.

To make the filling, beat the eggs lightly in a bowl, then add the sugar, syrup, salt and vanilla essence. Stir in the pecan nuts. Pour the mixture into the cooked flan case and bake in the pre-heated oven for 10 minutes. Reduce the oven temperature to 180°C/350°F/gas 4 again and bake for a further 35 minutes until set. You may need to cover the tart with foil to prevent any burning. Allow the pie to cool, then serve with clotted cream.

66 *Probably the most popular of classic American dishes – lovely tastes with a lovely texture.* **99**

Pecan Pie (see p. 205).

Sweet and Savoury Pancakes

It certainly doesn't have to be Pancake Day to make these pancakes, which can be made both savoury and sweet. Perhaps their most classic sweet use is the flambéed Crêpes Suzettes, great for a bit of show at your dinner party. Or, of course, you can use savoury ones in your main course Fillet of Venison Wellington (see p. 120).

SERVES 4

225 g (8 oz) plain flour
A pinch of salt
2 eggs
600 ml (1 pint) milk
50 g (2 oz) unsalted butter, melted
Vegetable oil
2 teaspoons chopped fresh parsley or
    herbs (optional)

Sift the flour and salt into a bowl. Beat the eggs into the milk, then whisk into the flour. Add the melted butter and whisk into the mix, which can now be used for sweet pancakes. For savoury pancakes, add the chopped herbs.

To cook the pancakes, pre-heat a 20 cm (8 in) or 15 cm (6 in) frying-pan; I prefer to make smaller pancakes. Lightly oil the pan and pour in some of the mixture, making sure the pan has only a thin layer of mix. Cook for 10–15 seconds until brown, turn in the pan and cook for a further 10–15 seconds. The pancake is now cooked. Keep warm while you make the remainder. Three small pancakes or two large will be enough for one portion.

Pancakes can be filled with anything you like – fruit or ice-cream for the sweet, seafood or vegetables for the savoury. Pancakes to be filled can, of course, be prepared in advance and then simply microwaved for 1–2 minutes to heat them through.

Apple Pancakes

I'm using apples for these filled pancakes, but pears or any other fruit can be used. There are also a few other additions you can make, some of which I list below.

SERVES 4

1 quantity Sweet Pancakes (see left)
6 ripe apples
50 g (2 oz) unsalted butter
50 g (2 oz) icing sugar

Peel, core and chop two of the apples and cook in half the butter and sugar until puréed. Peel and quarter the remaining apples then cut each quarter into four or five slices. Melt the remaining butter and toss the apple slices in this for a few minutes until just softening. Add the apple purée and bring to the simmer. The filling is now ready.

Allowing three pancakes per portion, divide the purée between the pancakes and either fold them in half or in quarters. Sit them in bowls and sprinkle with the remaining icing sugar. They can now be glazed under a hot grill to give a crispy topping. You can serve them with clotted or double cream, but here are a few ideas of how to enhance all the flavours.

1 When making the purée, some calvados or reduced sweet cider can be added.
2 Serve the pancakes with home-made Apple Sorbet (see p. 200) or Vanilla Ice-cream (see p. 182).
3 Add calvados or reduced cider to some Anglaise Sauce (see p. 220) to serve as a sauce.
4 For the ultimate dessert, serve a calvados anglaise and Apple Sorbet with the pancakes.

*Banana and Pecan Nut Bread
(see p. 213) and
Gingerbread Cake (see
p. 212).*

Gingerbread Cake

This gingerbread can be served as a warm pudding or simply as a cold cake (see pp. 210–11). I like to use it as both, and find that it eats really well with Clementine or Orange Sauce (see p. 221) and clotted cream.

SERVES 4

450 g (1 lb) plain flour
¾ tablespoon ground ginger
¾ tablespoon baking powder
1 teaspoon bicarbonate of soda
A pinch of salt
25 g (1 oz) demerara sugar
100 g (4 oz) unsalted butter
100 g (4 oz) treacle
100 g (4 oz) golden syrup
1 egg
150 ml (5 fl oz) milk

Pre-heat the oven to 180°C/350°F/gas 4 and grease and line a 900 g (2 lb) loaf tin.

Mix together the flour, ginger, baking powder, bicarbonate of soda and salt in a bowl. Warm the sugar, butter, treacle and golden syrup together in a pan. Beat the egg into the milk, then mix all the ingredients in the bowl. The gingerbread is made. Pour the mixture into the lined tin and spread evenly. Simply bake in the pre-heated oven for 1¼ hours. Remove from the tin and leave to stand for a few minutes before serving warm, or just leave to cool.

Banana and Pecan Nut Bread

This can be served as an afternoon teacake (see pp. 210–11), or eats very well with clotted cream and warm Chocolate Sauce (see p. 221) as a pudding.

MAKES 1 × 450 g (1 lb) loaf

3 large ripe bananas
225 g (8 oz) self-raising flour
A pinch of salt
175 g (6 oz) caster sugar
100 g (4 oz) unsalted butter, softened
2 eggs
2 tablespoons golden syrup
50 g (2 oz) pecan nuts

Pre-heat the oven to 160°C/325°F/gas 3 and grease a 450 g (1 lb) loaf tin.

Peel and mash the bananas in a bowl then add the remaining ingredients and beat vigorously for a minute to make sure they are well combined. Spoon the mixture into the loaf tin and spread it to the sides. Sprinkle the top with the pecan nuts and bake in the pre-heated oven for 1¼ hours until well risen and firm to the touch. Leave the loaf to rest for 10–15 minutes in the tin and then turn on to a cooling rack and leave to rest and become cold or just serve warm as a pudding.

Vanilla Sponge
(Genoise)

This sponge can be used for many things: cakes, gâteaux, trifles or Manchester Pudding are just a few.

MAKES 1 × 20 cm (8 in) sponge

6 eggs
175 g (6 oz) caster sugar, flavoured with
    vanilla (see p. 182)
175 g (6 oz) plain flour, sifted
75 g (3 oz) unsalted butter, melted

Pre-heat the oven to 200°C/400°F/gas 6, grease a 20 cm (8 in) round cake tin and dust with flour.

Whisk the eggs and sugar together in a bowl over a pan of hot water. Continue to whisk until the mixture has doubled in volume and is light and creamy. Remove from the heat and continue to whisk until cold and thick. This is called the ribbon stage as the mixture will trail off the whisk in ribbons when you lift it out of the mixture. Lightly fold in the flour and melted butter. Gently pour the mix into the prepared tin and bake in the pre-heated oven for about 30 minutes. The easiest way to test is with a skewer, which will come out clean when the sponge is ready.

Allow to cool for 10 minutes in the tin and then turn out on to a wire rack.

Breakfast Muesli

This is a recipe I couldn't resist. It really is good just with cold milk for breakfast, or it can be mixed with chocolate to make a biscuit to be eaten with ice-cream and Anglaise Sauce (see p. 220) as a pudding.

MAKES 1 kg (2¼ lb)

350 g (12 oz) jumbo oats
100 g (4 oz) sunflower seeds
100 g (4 oz) wheatgerm
75 g (3 oz) demerara sugar
75 ml (3 fl oz) olive oil
100 g (4 oz) clear honey

40 g (1½ oz) dried apple, coarsely chopped
40 g (1½ oz) dried apricots, coarsely chopped
75 g (3 oz) flaked almonds, toasted
75 g (3 oz) All-Bran (optional)
100 g (4 oz) raisins

Pre-heat the oven to 180°C/350°F/gas 4.

Place the first six ingredients in a small roasting tray, mix together, then cook in the pre-heated oven, stirring regularly, for 15–20 minutes until golden brown. Remove from the oven and leave to cool, stirring all the time.

When cold, stir in the remaining ingredients. Mix them together well, then store in an airtight container. This will keep for up to two weeks. The muesli is now ready to use.

Crunchy Chocolate Muesli Biscuits

MAKES about 30 biscuits

225 g (8 oz) plain or milk chocolate
½ quantity Breakfast Muesli (see above)

Melt the chocolate in a bowl over a pan of hot water. Remove from the heat and leave to cool for a few minutes. Stir in enough muesli so that the mixture will be just held together by the chocolate.

To make sweets, spoon the mixture into small paper cases, or just on to a tray. Cool, then chill until set.

To make biscuits, the mix can be spread on to a tray lined with waxed paper. When set, it can be cut into fingers. Alternatively, spread the warm melted chocolate on to waxed paper, then sprinkle the muesli liberally over the top. Set this in the fridge, and the resulting biscuits could almost be called 'country florentines'. When set, the mix can be cut into rounds or fingers and served with home-made ice-creams.

Puff Pastry

This recipe is used for the Apple Tarts (see p. 200), Home-made Pasties (see p. 134), and could also be used for a steak and kidney pie. It's very simple to do, just place the steak and kidney filling from the pudding recipe (see p. 122) in a pie-dish, cover with the puff pastry and bake in a pre-heated oven at 200°C/400°F/gas 6 for about 30 minutes until the pastry is golden and crisp.

MAKES about 450 g (1 lb)

225 g (8 oz) unsalted butter
225 g (8 oz) strong plain flour
A pinch of salt
150 ml (5 fl oz) cold water
A few drops of lemon juice

Cut off 50 g (2 oz) of the butter, melt it then leave it to cool. The remaining 175 g (6 oz) block should be left out to soften. Sift the flour and salt together into a large bowl and make a well in the centre. Pour the water, lemon juice and cooled, melted butter into the well in the flour and gently fold in the flour to make a pliable dough. Allow to rest for 20 minutes.

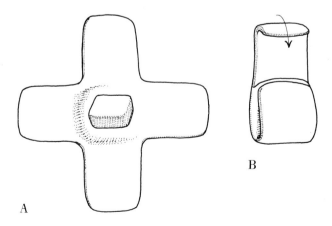

A   B

On a lightly floured board, roll the pastry from four sides, leaving a lump in the centre. The dough should look like a crossroads. The remaining block of butter should have softened to a similar texture to the dough; it should be easy to roll without melting and not so hard that it will break the pastry.

Sit the butter on the centre lump of the dough (A) and fold over each pastry flap (B). Pat the pastry into a 30 × 15 cm (12 × 6 in) rectangle and leave to rest in the fridge for 10–15 minutes.

Roll the pastry lengthways to make it double in length to about 60 cm (24 in) but the same width (C). Fold in both ends to the centre (D) and then fold once more (E). This is called a double turn and should be completed a further 3 times, each time rolling out the same length and then finishing with a double turn. Always roll with the folded edge on the left, and always leave to rest for 20–30 minutes in the fridge before each turn. The pastry should now be rested for a minimum of 30 minutes in the fridge before using.

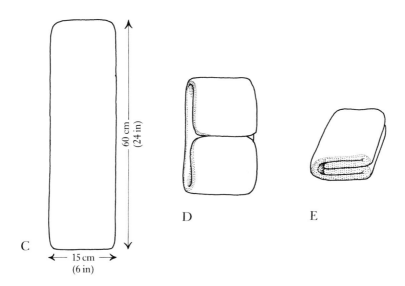

C   60 cm (24 in)   15 cm (6 in)   D   E

Palmier Biscuits

When using puff pastry for different recipes there are always some trimmings left over which quite often just get thrown away. Well, here is a way of using them all up and making great biscuits to serve with Cappuccino Mousse (see p. 172), Vanilla Ice-cream (see p. 182), sorbets (see p. 184) or petits fours.

Puff pastry trimmings, rolled together
Icing sugar

Pre-heat the oven to 220°C/425°F/gas 7 and dampen a baking sheet.

Sprinkle icing sugar liberally on to the work surface and give the pastry one more double turn with the sugar. Rest in the fridge for 15 minutes.

Once chilled, sprinkle more icing sugar on to the surface and roll out the pastry to 3 mm (⅛ in) thick. Trim the edges. If this makes a large square, then cut the pastry in half (A) and double turn each strip (B). Rest in the fridge or freezer for 20 minutes until set.

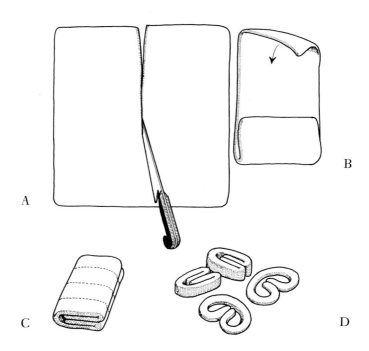

When set, cut each folded strip into pieces about 5 mm (¼ in) thick (C), lay them flat on the work surface, dust with more icing sugar and flatten lightly with a rolling pin (D). Lay them on the baking sheet and cook in the pre-heated oven for about 5 minutes. Turn them over on the tray and cook for a further 5 minutes until golden and crisp. Leave to cool on a wire rack. The biscuits will keep in an airtight container for 24 hours, but are best eaten on the same day.

Sweet (and Savoury) Pastry

This sweet pastry cooks to a light and crumbly texture and, of course, if you omit the icing sugar and vanilla you have an instant savoury pastry for all your flans and pies. In the Glazed Lemon Tart recipe (see p. 202), I use this basic recipe with the addition of lemon zest for extra taste. For a shorter pastry texture replace half of the buttter with lard.

MAKES about 800 g (1¾ lb)

450 g (1 lb) plain flour
150 g (5 oz) icing sugar
A pinch of salt
1 vanilla pod (optional)
225 g (8 oz) unsalted butter
1 egg
1 tablespoon milk

Sift the flour, icing sugar and salt together. Split the vanilla pod, if using, scrape out the seeds and mix into the flour. This is an optional extra but it gives a wonderful taste to the pastry for any pudding flans.

Rub in the butter to give a breadcrumb texture. Beat the egg with the milk and work into the mix to form a dough. Wrap in cling film and leave to rest in the fridge for 20–30 minutes before using.

Anglaise (Fresh Custard) Sauce

This so-called Anglaise Sauce is really just a fresh custard sauce. It's great with steamed puddings, tarts and trifles.

MAKES 750 ml (1¼ pints)

8 egg yolks
75 g (3 oz) caster sugar flavoured with
    vanilla (see p. 182)
1 vanilla pod, split (optional)
300 ml (10 fl oz) milk
300 ml (10 fl oz) double cream

Beat the egg yolks and sugar together in a bowl until well blended. Scrape the insides of the vanilla pod into the milk and cream and bring to the boil. Sit the bowl over a pan of hot water and whisk the cream into the egg yolks and sugar. As the egg yolks cook, the custard will thicken. Keep stirring until it starts to coat the back of a spoon, then remove the bowl from the heat and stir the sauce occasionally until cool. The custard is now ready to serve.

It can also be brought back up to heat over a pan of hot water, but must never boil. If that happens, the sauce will separate.

Coffee Sauce

The custard recipe above can also be used to create rich coffee sauce which tastes good with the Cappuccino Mousse (see p. 172) or a home-made Vanilla Ice-cream (see p. 182).

Just replace the vanilla pod with 2 teaspoons of fresh, ground coffee, and bring to the boil with the milk and cream. Cook as above, and when ready, pour through a sieve to remove any coarse granules. The sauce will have taken on a light coffee colour with very fine granules left in.

Chocolate Sauce

This sauce goes very well with pear sorbet, banana ice-cream, Vanilla Ice-cream (see p. 182), or a steamed chocolate pudding.

MAKES about 350 ml (12 fl oz)

225 g (8 oz) plain chocolate
150 ml (5 fl oz) milk
75 ml (3 fl oz) double cream
40 g (1½ oz) caster sugar

Melt the chocolate in a bowl over a pan of hot water. Do not allow it to get too hot or this will make it grainy. Boil the milk, double cream and sugar together and stir into the chocolate. Allow the mixture to cool, stirring occasionally. The sauce is now finished and ready to use.

To enrich the taste and consistency, 25 g (1 oz) of unsalted butter can be added while the sauce is still warm.

Clementine or Orange Sauce

This is a good sauce for ice-creams, sorbets (see p. 184), Gingerbread Cake (see p. 212), or even Cappuccino Mousse (see p. 172).

MAKES about 600 ml (1 pint)

2.25 kg (5 lb) clementines or oranges
15 g (½ oz) arrowroot
Icing sugar to taste

Squeeze the juice from the clementines or oranges then push the juice through a sieve. This should leave you with at least 600 ml (1 pint) of juice. Bring to the boil and boil until reduced by half; in fact, whatever quantity of juice you have, always reduce it by half. Mix the arrowroot with a little water to soften it, then add it to the reduced juice a little at a time, stirring continuously until you have a sauce that will lightly coat the back of a spoon. Allow the sauce barely to simmer for 3–4 minutes. Remove from the heat and leave to cool.

When the sauce is cold, it should be a rich orange colour and have a full taste. If you feel it needs to be a little sweeter, just stir in some icing sugar.

Sauces, Stocks and Pickles

It's in this section that you will find all the bits and pieces – the stocks, sauces, gravies, dressings, chutneys etc. – that are so important to good cooking. It's a shame to lump them together almost as an afterthought, because they are so basic to so many of the recipes, but it is the most convenient way to place them. You will find some other similar recipes in other chapters of the book, as I see some of the recipes as an integral part of a particular main course or starter.

ABOVE *Grilled Mackerel with Stewed Tomatoes, Pesto and Onions (see p. 44).*
LEFT *Foreground, Chicken Liver Parfait (see p. 62), back right, Grape Chutney (see p. 251), back left, Piccalilli (see p. 252).*

Vinegar

Malt vinegar is probably the best-known, especially for sprinkling on your fish and chips! Malt vinegar is made from malted barley (as, of course, is whisky), and gets its colour from caramel. The strongest of vinegars, it is used mostly for pickling, and I've used it here in a chutney recipe where it helps achieve the right acidity for the ingredients. Don't use it in basic dressings, as its strength is just too much for salads.

Red and white wine vinegars are the ones to use for most general dressings and purposes. Red wine vinegar is the best. Wine vinegars are allowed to mature slowly in barrels until the vinegars have turned the alcohol into acetic acid. They can be made more swiftly by heating, but this tends to destroy some of the flavours.

Balsamic vinegar must be the most-used vinegar in modern cookery, which doesn't surprise me as it really is astounding. There are many cheap copies on the market, which aren't worth buying. Real balsamic vinegar is made from Trebbiano grapes, and should be a mimimum of five years old to have any true flavour. The older it gets, the better and stronger it tastes but, of course, the more expensive it is to buy. Twelve-year-old balsamic is a great medium and although it's pricey, you need very little because of its immense flavour. Some balsamics can be as old as forty years, but this is very rare, and you'll probably have to wait another forty years to try one!

Oils

The oils that I generally use are olive oil (extra virgin) and ground-nut (peanut) oil.

Ground-nut oil is a very basic oil which is used in France (*huile à la arachide*) as a base in most dressings and in frying. It's very similar to sunflower oil, and has quite a bland flavour. In the basic dressing here, I mix it with olive oil, which prevents the dressing from being too overpowering. It is also cheaper to make, and works well on all simple salads.

Virgin olive oil is an oil from the first pressing, which is totally pure, without any heating or chemical processing. The 'extra' in front applies to its low acidity grade. Extra virgin oil has 1 per cent acidity, which is the lowest and the best.

Alternative Stocks and Sauces

These may look really hard work, but they're not at all. They may not always be practical to make in the home, though, so I've been out doing some homework on stocks and sauces, in search of some good commercial alternatives to make the cooking of some of my dishes a little easier.

Fish and Chicken Stocks

Alternatives to these can be found in the chill cabinet of most Sainsbury's and other quality supermarkets. They are sold in plastic tubs, each containing about 284 ml (about 9–10 fl oz). The beauty of these is a) they taste great, b) they have good colour and jelly texture, and c) they are sold as stocks ready to use. They really are the best I've found, but if you can't get hold of them, there are also some good-quality stock cubes.

Beef and Veal *Jus*

In the basic recipe, these start out as stocks, and then for use in other recipes, they are reduced to a sauce consistency. I've found a sauce which will cut out all of this, and is an instant *jus* to use as a base sauce in many of the recipes asking for veal or beef *jus*. Madeira Wine Gravy is made by Crosse & Blackwell in their Bonne Cuisine range, and should be available in just about every supermarket or good grocery shop. The Madeira flavour gives it good body and, when made, it has a lovely glossy finish. I've tried it with the Braised Oxtails and in Onion Gravy, and my only advice is to mix it with 600 ml (1 pint) of water instead of 300 ml (10 fl oz). This way, when slow braising or stewing, there's room for reduction and it won't become too thick. If you are cooking oxtail for four to six people, then I would use two packets and 1.2 litres (2 pints) of water. This would make a stock consistency, but once the meat is cooked, you'll finish with a good, rich sauce.

Other Sauces and Ingredients

Another sauce which I found very good is in the same range as the Madeira gravy above, the hollandaise sauce. I use hollandaise in the sardine recipe on page 45, so if you are unsure about making it, give this bought one a try; it's so easy.

There's only one other small suggestion. If you don't have any chillies for the Rouille recipe on p. 24, then use the chilli sauce made by Maggi in its place. It's sold in bottles and can be added slowly to taste.

As for dried pastas and ready-made pastry, all varieties can be found easily in local shops. If you're lucky enough to have a good delicatessen nearby, then perhaps buy your pasta there; it's often made on the premises.

I hope these few suggestions will help. It's always good to have a go at making your own stocks, sauces, *jus* and pasta, but cooking has to be practical and for regular use the products mentioned above will help tremendously. I certainly think they will make life for you an awful lot easier.

Fish Stock

To make a good fish stock, you'll need a friendly fishmonger. Turbot and sole bones produce the best stock, giving a good, full taste and clear jelly-like finish. The stock is good for poaching fish and for making fish soups and sauces. (For information on ready-made alternatives see p. 225.)

MAKES about 2 litres (3½ pints)

1 large onion, sliced
1 leek, sliced
2 celery sticks, sliced
50 g (2 oz) unsalted butter
A few fresh parsley stalks
1 bay leaf
6 black peppercorns
900 g (2 lb) turbot or sole bones, washed
300 ml (10 fl oz) dry white wine
2.25 litres (4 pints) water

Sweat the sliced vegetables in the butter without colouring. Add the parsley stalks, bay leaf and peppercorns. Chop the fish bones, making sure there are no blood clots left on them. Add to the vegetables and continue to cook for a few minutes. Add the wine and boil to reduce until almost dry. Add the water and bring to the simmer. Allow to simmer for 20 minutes, then drain through a sieve. The stock is now ready to use, or to store for a few days in the fridge.

Chicken Stock

Chicken stock is one of our most important bases. It's used for most soups and many cream sauces. It's also very simple to make. I'm sure your local butcher will help you out with some chicken bones. If not, then cook a boiling fowl with vegetables in water and you will have an instant tasty stock and the bird to eat as well. If you do not have a large stock pot, you can easily reduce the quantities. (For information on ready-made alternatives see p. 225.)

MAKES 2.25 litres (4 pints)

2 onions, chopped
2 celery sticks, chopped
2 leeks, chopped
25 g (1 oz) unsalted butter
1 garlic clove, crushed
1 bay leaf
1 sprig of fresh thyme
A few black peppercorns
1.8 kg (4 lb) chicken carcasses, chopped
3.4 litres (6 pints) water

In a large stock pot (about 8.5 litres (15 pint) capacity), lightly soften the vegetables in the butter without colouring. Add the garlic, bay leaf, thyme, peppercorns and chopped carcasses. Cover with the cold water and bring to the simmer, skimming all the time. Allow the stock to simmer for 2–3 hours, then drain through a sieve. The stock is now ready to use and will keep well chilled or frozen.

Vegetable Stock

This stock is a great substitute for chicken and fish stock in lots of the recipes in this book. It's easy to make and works very well in vegetarian risottos or soups. This is a very basic recipe, but many other flavours can be added, such as mushrooms or tomatoes – both would add different tastes for different dishes.

MAKES about 1 litre (1¾ pints)

225 g (8 oz) carrots
225 g (8 oz) celery sticks
1 large onion
1 leek
50 g (2 oz) unsalted butter
1 bay leaf
1 sprig of fresh thyme
1 small garlic clove, crushed
1.2 litres (2 pints) water
Salt and freshly ground black pepper

Cut the vegetables roughly into 1 cm (½ in) dice. Melt the butter in a large pan and add the diced vegetables, herbs and garlic. Cover with a lid and cook over a low heat for 6–8 minutes, stirring from time to time. Add the water, bring to the simmer and cook for 20–30 minutes. Remove from the heat and allow the vegetables to stand in the stock until cool.

Pour the stock through a sieve, squeezing out all the juices from the vegetables but not puréeing them. Taste, and season with salt and pepper. The stock is now ready to use. If you find it's not strong enough, then just boil to reduce it until you are happy with the taste. Check again for seasoning after reduction.

*Noodles in Creamy Mushroom
Sauce to be served with
chicken breasts (see p. 92).
The mushroom sauce is made
with chicken stock
(see p. 228).*

Veal or Beef Stock and *Jus*

This stock is a base to a lot of cooking, and really holds the essence of a good dish. Reading this recipe may well make you want to think twice about it, but it is worth making and so satisfying once made. It will give you great sauces and, of course, will store well in your freezer, so go on, have a go! It is best started in the morning, which will allow the stock to cook throughout the day.

If this really is too much, then a lot of good gravy bases can be found but do use them carefully, not making them too thick and strong. (For information on ready-made alternatives see p. 225.)

MAKES 4.5–5.5 litres (8–10 pints) stock
or 600 ml–1.2 litres (1–2 pints) *jus*

3 onions, halved	3 celery sticks, coarsely chopped
2–3 tablespoons water	1 leek, chopped
2.25 kg (5 lb) veal or beef bones	3–4 tomatoes, chopped
225 g (8 oz) veal or beef trimmings from the butcher	1 garlic clove, halved
	1 bay leaf
225 g (8 oz) carrots, coarsely chopped	1 sprig of fresh thyme

Pre-heat the oven to 110°C/225°F/gas ¼–½. Lay the onion halves flat in a roasting tray with the water. Place the onion into the very cool oven and allow to slowly caramelize until they have totally softened and coloured. This process will take 1–2 hours. The sugars in the onions will slowly cook and give a wonderful taste. Pop the onions into a large stock pot and leave on one side. Increase the oven temperature to 200°C/400°F/gas 6.

Place all the bones and trimmings in a roasting tray and roast for about 30 minutes until well coloured. Roast the chopped carrots and celery in another roasting tray for about 20 minutes until lightly coloured.

When ready, add the bones, trimmings and vegetables to the onions in the pot, along with the leeks, tomatoes, garlic, bay leaf and thyme. Fill the pot with cold water – you'll need about 5.5–6.5 litres (10–12 pints). Bring the stock to the simmer and skim off any impurities. Allow to cook for 6–8 hours, and with this you will achieve the maximum taste. If it seems to be reducing too quickly during cooking, top up with cold water.

When ready, drain and discard the bones and vegetables. This is now your veal stock, and you can cool it and freeze it in convenient quantities.

Or you can make a veal *jus* with the stock. Allow the liquid to boil and reduce down to 600 ml–1.2 litres (1–2 pints), skimming all the time. The stock should be thick and of a sauce consistency. Make sure that you taste all the time during reduction. If the sauce tastes right but is not thick enough, thicken it lightly with cornflour. (Of course, I do hope that won't be necessary!) You now have a veal *jus*, a classic sauce.

Onion Gravy

I use this simple gravy to accompany the Home-made Pork Sausages on p. 116 and also serve it with Calves' Liver with Onion Gravy and Mashed Potatoes (see p. 102), a dish that has become a bit of a classic. The gravy is also a vital component of my faggot recipe on p. 104.

SERVES 4

8 onions, thinly sliced
2 tablespoons water
600 ml (1 pint) Veal *Jus* (see left) or
    bought alternative (see p. 225)

Place the sliced onions in a pan with the water and cook very slowly, stirring all the time. The sugar from the onions will slowly caramelize and become brown and sweet-tasting. The process will take 1½–2 hours.

Add the veal *jus* and simmer for a further 30 minutes. The gravy will now be even richer in taste and colour with a lovely shiny finish.

OVERLEAF
*'Saucing the plates' for, left, Grilled
Sardine Fillets on Tomato Toasts
(see p. 45) and, right,
Calves' Liver with Onion Gravy
and Mashed Potatoes
(see p. 102).*

Red Wine Sauce

This sauce tastes good with almost any meat – chicken, beef, pork, veal – and even eats well with baked fish.

Makes about 1.2 litres (2 pints)

4 shallots, chopped
1 large carrot, chopped
2 celery sticks, chopped
25 g (1 oz) unsalted butter
1 garlic clove, crushed
1 bay leaf
1 sprig of fresh thyme
225 g (8 oz) beef skirt or trimmings from
    the butcher (optional)
1 tablespoon olive oil (optional)
1 bottle red wine
1.2 litres (2 pints) Veal *Jus* (see p. 232)
    or bought alternative (see p. 225)
Salt and freshly ground white pepper

In a large pan, cook the chopped vegetables in a little butter with the garlic and herbs, allowing them to colour. In a frying-pan, fry the meat, if used, in the oil, colouring on all sides, then add the meat to the vegetables. Pour the red wine into the frying-pan to release any flavours from the trimmings. Scrape and stir, then pour the wine on to the meat and vegetables and boil to reduce until almost dry.

Add the veal *jus* and bring to the simmer, skim off any impurities, then simmer the sauce gently for 30 minutes. Pass through a sieve, squeezing all the juices from the vegetables and meat. Check for seasoning, and you now have a rich, glistening red wine sauce.

Curry Cream Sauce

This recipe will provide a slightly yellow, creamy curry sauce with just enough strength to flavour the kedgeree (see p. 46). Any left-over sauce can be kept in the fridge for a few days. It's good added to any curry.

MAKES 600 ml (1 pint)

1 onion, chopped
1 carrot, chopped
½ leek, chopped
2 celery sticks, chopped
1 garlic clove, chopped
½ teaspoon ground ginger or a small
    piece of fresh root ginger, grated
A few coriander seeds (optional)
A few cardamom seeds (optional)
A few black peppercorns
50 g (2 oz) unsalted butter
2 teaspoons medium curry powder
600 ml (1 pint) Chicken Stock (see
    p. 228) or Vegetable Stock (see
    p. 229)
300 ml (10 fl oz) double cream
Salt and freshly ground white pepper

Cook all the chopped vegetables, garlic and spices in the butter for 10 minutes. Add the curry powder and continue to cook for 15 minutes. Add the chicken stock and bring to the simmer. Simmer the stock until reduced by half. Now add the cream and cook for 10–15 minutes. Season with salt and pepper. Push the sauce through a sieve; it is now

Tomato and Onion Flavoured Gravy
to accompany Jambonette de Volaille
(see p. 96).

Tomato and Onion Flavoured Gravy

This sauce has a delicious variety of flavours, and goes particularly well with lamb and chicken dishes.

MAKES 1.5 litres (2½ pints)

4 onions, sliced
1–2 tablespoons water
8 tomatoes, chopped
1 garlic clove, crushed
1 small sprig of fresh rosemary
8 fresh basil leaves
300 ml (10 fl oz) Noilly Prat or white
    vermouth
300 ml (10 fl oz) dry white wine
1.2 litres (2 pints) Veal *Jus* (see p. 232)
    or bought alternative (see p. 225)

Cook the sliced onions with the water very slowly until they have naturally caramelized, stirring occasionally. This will take at least an hour. Add the tomatoes, garlic and herbs and continue to cook for 15–20 minutes until the tomatoes are soft. Pour in the Noilly Prat or vermouth and the white wine and boil to reduce until almost dry. Add the *jus*, bring to the simmer and cook for 30 minutes. Blitz using a hand blender or liquidizer. This will thicken the sauce and help it take on lots more tastes. Pass through a sieve and serve.

Tomato or Red Pepper Coulis

You can use the same recipe to make either a tomato coulis (see p.151), or a red pepper version. For a red pepper coulis, replace 350 g (12 oz) of the tomatoes with an equal weight of seeded red peppers, then follow the same procedure to make the coulis.

MAKES about 900 ml (1½ pints)

1 large onion, chopped
2 celery sticks, chopped
1 large carrot, chopped
1 garlic clove, crushed
A few fresh basil or tarragon leaves or a pinch of dried tarragon
1 sprig of fresh thyme or a pinch of dried thyme
2 tablespoons olive oil
50 g (2 oz) unsalted butter

150 ml (5 fl oz) dry white wine
450 g (1 lb) tomatoes, chopped
300 ml (10 fl oz) Chicken Stock (see p.228) or Vegetable Stock (see p.229)
1 tablespoon tomato purée
Salt and freshly ground white pepper
A few drops of Spicing Essence (see p.242) (optional)

Cook the chopped onion, celery and carrot with the garlic and herbs in the olive oil and butter for a few minutes until softened. Add the white wine and boil to reduce until almost dry. Add the chopped tomatoes and cook for a few minutes, then add the stock and tomato purée, bring to the simmer, cover with a lid and continue to cook for 20 minutes. Liquidize the sauce then push it through a sieve to give a smooth sauce consistency. If the sauce is a little thick, add more stock to reach the right consistency. Season to taste with salt and pepper. The coulis is now ready. To make the sauce more spicy, add a few drops of the spicing essence at a time, if using, whisking and tasting until you have the flavour you want.

Spicy Tomato Sauce

This sauce goes so well with seafood of all types. It's almost like eating a loose, spicy tomato chutney. Once made, it can be kept chilled for up to two weeks.

MAKES about 450 g (1 lb)

85 ml (3 fl oz) olive oil
3 shallots or 2 onions, finely
  chopped
2 garlic cloves, crushed
A few fresh basil, thyme and
  tarragon leaves

900 g (2 lb) tomatoes, skinned and
  seeded
2 tablespoons red wine vinegar
1 teaspoon caster sugar
Salt and freshly ground white pepper
2–3 drops Tabasco sauce

Warm the olive oil in a pan and add the chopped shallots or onions, the garlic and the herbs. It's best to have the herbs in sprigs, as these can then be easily removed at the end of cooking. Allow the shallots and herbs to cook for 4–5 minutes until tender.

Cut the tomato flesh into 5 mm (¼ in) dice and add to the shallots. Have the pan on a very low heat, just on a light simmer, and cook for about 45 minutes. The sauce may cook a little quicker, or take a little longer – this will really depend on the water content of the tomatoes. After 45 minutes, add the wine vinegar and sugar and cook for a further 15 minutes. The tomatoes should have taken on an almost lumpy sauce texture; if the sauce is very thick, simply fold in a little more olive oil. Allow to cool until just warm then season with salt, pepper and Tabasco. The sauce is now ready.

Rouille

MAKES about 300 ml (10 fl oz)

1 red pepper, seeded and chopped
1 small dried or fresh chilli pepper,
  seeded and chopped
2 garlic cloves, crushed

50 g (2 oz) fresh white breadcrumbs
1 egg yolk
Salt
150 ml (5 fl oz) extra virgin olive oil

Place the pepper and chilli in a food processor or liquidizer with the garlic, breadcrumbs, egg yolk and salt and blitz until smooth. With the motor still running, slowly add the olive oil as if making mayonnaise. When all the oil has been added, push the sauce through a sieve. It can be kept in the fridge for a couple of days without spoiling.

Plum Purée Sauce

This sauce has a wonderful, spicy plum flavour. Use it with a confit (see p. 98) or with Chinese dishes. It can simply be added to a basic jus *to make a rich spicy sauce.*

MAKES about 600–900 ml (1–1½ pints)

150 ml (5 fl oz) malt vinegar
50 g (2 oz) demerara sugar
1 shallot, chopped
450 g (1 lb) red plums, stoned and
    chopped
75 ml (2½ fl oz) Madeira
75 ml (2½ fl oz) port
Juice of ½ orange

Juice of ½ lemon
Juice of ½ lime
1 tablespoon redcurrant jelly
A pinch of five-spice powder
1 muslin bag containing 4 cloves,
    ½ cinnamon stick, 2 star anise
    and a few coriander seeds

Boil the vinegar and sugar together then add the chopped shallot and plums and cook for 5 minutes. Add the muslin bag and the remaining ingredients and cook slowly for 1 hour. Remove the muslin bag and liquidize the sauce. Push through a sieve to make a purée. The sauce is now ready and can be kept in airtight jars in the fridge almost indefinitely.

Spicing Essence

I think this little trick comes from Escoffier's days; it is often used for spicing up a sauce or other dish. It was also occasionally used to mask the flavours of a meat that wasn't quite right! Well, I'm glad to say that I use it purely for enhancing flavours, and it works its magic particularly with Tomato or Red Pepper Coulis (see p. 240).

MAKES about 150 ml (5 fl oz)

50 g (2 oz) demerara sugar
150 ml (5 fl oz) malt vinegar

Simply dissolve the sugar in the vinegar then boil for a few minutes until reduced to a syrup. It is now ready to use, and only a few drops are needed to spice your sauces. After that, it can be kept in an airtight jar in the fridge for as long as you like.

Lemon Butter Sauce

This is one of the simplest possible sauces, which has a silky texture and just enough acidity for the Salmon Fish Cakes (see p. 88). It goes well with cod, too (see p. 74).

SERVES 4–6

225 g (8 oz) unsalted butter
Juice of 1 lemon
50 ml (2 fl oz) Chicken Stock (see p. 228)
   or Vegetable Stock (see p. 229)
Salt and freshly ground white pepper

Chop the butter into 1 cm (½ in) pieces and put into a pan with the lemon juice and chicken stock. Bring to the simmer, whisking all the time. Do not allow the sauce to boil or the butter will separate. If it's too thick add more stock and if you like a sharper taste add more lemon juice. Season and serve immediately. To give a creamier texture, simply blitz the sauce with an electric hand blender.

Pesto Sauce

This is an Italian classic, although the French have a similar version called pistou. *It is a paste made from pine nuts, basil, garlic, olive oil and Parmesan cheese. It can easily be found in most delicatessens or supermarkets, but I'm going to give you a very simple recipe here. I make it without the Parmesan, which isn't needed for all of my dishes. I like to use it in soups, sauces and dressings.*

MAKES about 300 ml (10 fl oz)

25 g (1 oz) pine nuts
150 ml (5 fl oz) extra virgin olive oil
2 small garlic cloves, crushed
3 bunches of fresh basil, stalks removed
Salt and freshly ground white pepper

Very lightly colour the pine nuts in the olive oil, then remove from the heat. Add the garlic and leave to go cold. Pour the mixture into a food processor or liquidizer, add the basil leaves and blitz to a paste and season with salt and pepper. This paste can now be put in a jar and kept in the fridge for a few days.

Hollandaise Sauce

This is a French classic. It can be bought ready-made, but I'm going to give you two ways of making it. Both taste very good.

RECIPE 1: *The Classic*

225 g (8 oz) unsalted butter
2 tablespoons malt or white wine
   vinegar
6 white peppercorns, lightly crushed
1 tablespoon water
2 egg yolks
Salt and cayenne or freshly ground
   white pepper

Melt the butter in a pan then leave it to cool slightly so that it is just warm when added to the sauce; if it is too hot, the sauce will curdle. The butter will have separated, leaving all its solids in the base of your pan, which you can discard, so you will only be adding the butter oil to the sauce. This is clarified butter.

Boil the vinegar with the peppercorns until reduced by half. Add the cold water to cool and drain the reduction through a sieve into a bowl. Add the egg yolks and whisk together. Place the bowl over a pan of hot water and whisk to a sabayon. A sabayon is created by the cooking and thickening of the egg yolks. As they are whisked, they increase in volume to a cream consistency. When the yolks have reached this stage, remove the bowl from the heat and continue to whisk, slowly adding the warm, clarified butter. When all the clear butter has been added and whisked, the sauce should be a thick consistency which can now be seasoned with salt and cayenne or white pepper.

Should the hollandaise curdle, just take a tablespoon of warm water and very slowly whisk in the sauce. This should bring the sauce back to a nice consistency.

To increase the flavours of this sauce, a pinch of dried tarragon, basil and some chopped onion or shallot can be added to the reduction. This will leave you with a Sauce Béarnaise, which also goes well with meat dishes and even a plain grilled steak.

RECIPE 2: *The Easy Way*

225 g (8 oz) unsalted butter
2 egg yolks
1 tablespoon warm water
Juice of ½ lemon
Salt and cayenne or freshly ground
    white pepper

Clarify the butter as described in the classic recipe.

To make the sauce, just add the egg yolks to the water (this is a fake reduction) and make into a sabayon as in the previous recipe. Add the clarified butter, as before. When made, just add the lemon juice and seasoning.

This eats very nicely with Grilled Sardine Fillets (see p. 45).

So now you have two methods, the choice is yours!

Basic Vinaigrette

This basic recipe is very convenient. Once made, it can sit in your fridge and can be used at any time and for any dish you might fancy. The vinegar just gives a very slight sweetness to the taste.

MAKES 600 ml (1 pint)

300 ml (10 fl oz) extra virgin olive oil
    (French or Italian)
300 ml (10 fl oz) ground-nut oil
25 ml (1 fl oz) balsamic vinegar
1 bunch of fresh basil
½ bunch of fresh tarragon

3–4 sprigs of fresh thyme
12 black peppercorns, lightly crushed
3 shallots, finely chopped
2 garlic cloves, crushed
1 bay leaf
1 teaspoon coarse sea salt

Warm the olive and ground-nut oil together. Place all the remaining ingredients into a 750 ml (1¼ pint) bottle. Pour the oil into the bottle and close with a cork or screw top. For the best results, leave to marinate for a week which will allow all the flavours to enhance the oils. To help the dressing along, shake the bottle once a day. Taste for seasoning before using.

66 *Warming olive oil will help to release the maximum flavour.* *99*

A simple green salad dressed with Basic Vinaigrette (see p. 245).

Red Wine Vinaigrette

This is a very basic recipe. Many herbs can be added to the bottle to help infuse more flavours. The best to use, unchopped, are basil, tarragon and thyme. When the dressing is to be used, just add some chopped fresh chives, basil, thyme or tarragon to finish the dressing.

MAKES about 600 ml (1 pint)

4 shallots or 1 large onion, finely chopped	300 ml (10 fl oz) red wine vinegar
2 garlic cloves, crushed	2 teaspoons Dijon mustard
300 ml (10 fl oz) red wine	600 ml (1 pint) olive oil
	Salt and freshly ground black pepper

Mix the chopped shallots or onion with the garlic in a pan and add the red wine. Bring to the boil then reduce until almost dry. Add the red wine vinegar and boil to reduce by three-quarters. Remove the pan from the heat.

While the shallots are still warm, add the Dijon mustard and blend in with the olive oil. Season with salt and pepper. The dressing can now be left to cool and then bottled. Chilled, it keeps for two to four weeks.

Mayonnaise

This is another basic recipe, but so much nicer than bought mayonnaise. Use it with potatoes in a salad, or in my version of a club sandwich (see p. 64).

MAKES about 600 ml (1 pint)

3 egg yolks	Salt and freshly ground white pepper
1 tablespoon malt, white wine or balsamic vinegar	300 ml (10 fl oz) basic olive oil
A pinch of English or Dijon mustard	1 teaspoon hot water
	A few drops of lemon juice (optional)

Whisk the egg yolks, vinegar, mustard and seasonings together, then slowly add the olive oil, whisking continuously. When all the oil is added, finish with the water and correct the seasoning. A few drops of lemon juice can be added to enhance the taste.

Vierge Dressing

This dressing has a very different taste to the basic dressing, and lends itself best to fish dishes. I was first inspired to make it whilst staying at La Côte St Jacques in Joigny, France, in the mid 80s. The restaurant now has three Michelin stars. The dressing was served with a red mullet dish, so now I've got one of my own which is very simple to make (see p. 82).

MAKES 600 ml (1 pint)

600 ml (1 pint) extra virgin olive oil
  (French or Italian)
15 g (½ oz) coriander seeds, crushed
1 bunch of fresh tarragon

12 black peppercorns, crushed
4 shallots, chopped
2 garlic cloves, crushed
A pinch of sea salt

Warm the olive oil with the coriander seeds. Place the remaining ingredients into a 600 ml (1 pint) jar and pour the oil and coriander on top. Leave to marinate for 1 week, shaking the bottle daily.

Pasta Dough

This pasta dough can be used for lasagne, fettucine, ravioli and many more pasta dishes. You can make it by hand or in a food processor. It also freezes very well.

MAKES 450 g (1 lb) to serve 4

250 g (9 oz) fine semolina or plain flour
A pinch of salt
½ teaspoon olive oil
2 eggs
3 egg yolks

Mix the semolina or flour with the salt and olive oil, and mix well for 1 minute. Add the eggs and egg yolks and stir well until it becomes a dough. Knead the dough for 1–3 minutes until it has a smooth texture. It should now be wrapped in cling film and chilled for 30 minutes to rest.

The pasta is now ready to use. It can be rolled, cut and cooked straightaway, or cut and left to dry and used later. If dried, the pasta will always take a little longer to cook.

Chutneys and Pickles

I always like a pickle or chutney in a ham or cheese sandwich, or with my ploughman's lunch. Here are a few of my favourites, which certainly have their own distinctive flavours. The grape is sweet without being sickly, and the tomato is more savoury and sharp. The piccalilli is a combination of both but also has a spicy finish. One thing's for sure, they're all delicious.

You will need a large pan or preserving pan for making chutneys. The best jars to use for this are Kilner jars with rubber seals. If you are using a screw-top lid, keep the chutneys chilled and they'll last a lot longer. Do not use metal lids as they react with the acid in the vinegar.

Grape Chutney

This chutney (see pp. 222–3) improves with time and is delicious to serve with the Chicken Liver Parfait (see p. 62).

MAKES about 1.5 kg (3 lb)

10 Granny Smith or Golden Delicious apples, peeled, cored and chopped
2 onions, finely chopped
300 ml (10 fl oz) good balsamic vinegar
300 ml (10 fl oz) drinkable brandy

2.25 kg (5 lb) seedless white grapes, picked and washed
350 g (12 oz) demerara sugar
A pinch of salt
2 teaspoons mixed spice
2 teaspoons ground cinnamon
1 teaspoon ground ginger

Simmer the apples, onions, balsamic vinegar and brandy together in a preserving pan for 30 minutes. Stir in the grapes, sugar, salt and spices and continue to simmer for 1½–2 hours over a low heat until the mixture is thick and pulpy, stirring occasionally. Should the chutney still seem a little too liquid, boil on a high heat to allow the excess liquid to evaporate.

Let the chutney cool slightly then spoon into warm, sterile jars. Seal then label and store in a cool, dark place until needed.

Green Tomato Chutney

MAKES about 1.5 kg (3 lb)

2.25 kg (5 lb) green tomatoes, cut into 8
600 ml (1 pint) malt vinegar
5 large onions, finely chopped
225 g (8 oz) raisins
450 g (1 lb) sultanas

350 g (12 oz) demerara sugar
25 g (1 oz) salt
4 teaspoons mixed spice
4 teaspoons ground cinnamon
2 teaspoons ground ginger

Place the tomatoes in a preserving pan, add the vinegar and simmer over a low heat for 30 minutes. Add the onions, raisins and sultanas and continue to cook for a further 30 minutes. Add the sugar, salt and spices and simmer gently for 1½–2 hours until thick, stirring occasionally. Leave to cool slightly, then spoon into warm, sterile jars.

Piccalilli

This has to be one of the easiest pickle recipes that I make (see pp. 222–3). There are so many variations that you can try – different vegetables, mustards and vinegars. This pickle eats particularly well with oily fish such as mackerel and herrings; its acidity works against the oils and leaves a good, clean taste.

MAKES about 1.25 kg (3 lb)

1 cauliflower
3 large onions
8 large shallots, or 16 onions if
     unavailable
Salt and freshly ground white pepper
1 cucumber
600 ml (1 pint) white wine vinegar

300 ml (10 fl oz) malt vinegar
¼ teaspoon chopped dried chilli
350 g (12 oz) caster sugar
50 g (2 oz) English mustard
     powder
25 g (1 oz) ground turmeric
3 tablespoons cornflour

Cut the cauliflower into small florets. Peel and cut the onions and shallots into 1 cm (½ in) dice. Place in a bowl, sprinkle with 25 g (1 oz) of salt and leave to stand for 24 hours. Afterwards rinse in cold water and dry.

Peel and de-seed the cucumber and cut it into 1 cm (½ in) dice. Sprinkle with a little salt and leave to stand for 10–15 minutes. Rinse in cold water, then dry and add to the onions and cauliflower.

Boil the two vinegars together with the chilli and then leave to cool for 30 minutes. Strain through a sieve and discard the chilli.

Mix together the sugar and remaining dry ingredients in a bowl. When the vinegar is cool, mix a little of it with the dry ingredients. Bring the bulk of the vinegar back to the boil, pour into the sugar mixture, and whisk until it is all blended together. Bring this mixture back to the boil and cook for 3 minutes, then simply pour over the vegetables and mix well. Leave to cool. The piccalilli is now ready and can be put into jars and refrigerated, or served at once. It will keep refrigerated for at least a month.

Index

Page numbers in *italic* refer to the illustrations